Love Signs 1995

Virgo

For a further insight into what the future holds for you, CALL THE
SUNDAY EXPRESS ASTROLOGY LINES NOW:

The Secret of the Runes – see if the ancient spiritual tradition
of the Rune Stones can answer your questions: **0891-111-666**

The Vision of the Cards – the 53 cards tell your fortune. Let us
reveal their magic and see what the secret symbols of knowledge
may hold in store for you: **0891-111-667**

Calls cost 39p per minute cheap rate, 49p per minute at all other
times – prices correct at time of going to press

Sunday
EXPRESS

Love Signs 1995
Virgo

24 August – 23 September

ARROW

First published in 1994

1 3 5 7 9 8 6 4 2

First published in the United Kingdom in 1994
by Vermilion Arrow
an imprint of Ebury Press
Random House, 20 Vauxhall Bridge Road,
London SW1V 2SA

Random House Australia (Pty) Limited
20 Alfred Street, Milsons Point, Sydney,
New South Wales 2061, Australia

Random House New Zealand Limited
18 Poland Road, Glenfield,
Auckland 10, New Zealand

Random House South Africa (Pty) Limited
PO Box 337, Bergvlei, 2012 South Africa

Random House UK Limited Reg. No. 954009

A CIP record for this title is available from the British Library

ISBN 0099368811

Designed by Nigel Hazle
Typeset from author's disks by Clive Dorman & Co.
Printed and bound in Great Britain by
Cox & Wyman Ltd, Reading, Berks

Contents

Introduction

**Astrology is about *how* we are,
not *why* we are.**

This book aims to be a guide to what you might expect from people as lovers, partners and friends. It also gives you an insight into who you really are, and how others see you. The forecasts for October 1994 through to December 1995 reveal the *mood* of the month for your Sun sign in the areas of love, emotions, sex, leisure and friendship. It will give you a fresh insight into getting the best out of your relationships for the months ahead. Keep your eyes on the stars and the stars in your eyes, and you won't go far wrong.

Astrology makes no claims to prophecy. It is only a reflection of human psychology: a mirror of us all and the paths we take.

Sun signs divide and generalise, no more or less than any other approach to our existence. They do show the basic qualities we have in common, the emotions and feelings and intellect that we all share and how we use our personal map of life. The map of life is in all of us, and every individual has his or her unique chart. Some areas of our personality are more prominent than others, like on the map of the world, where oceans and continents can be highlighted, or mountains or rivers. Sometimes we project different continents on to that map, other countries of feeling or mentality that are not highlighted on our own personal chart, but are highlighted in someone else.

There are so many other points involved in your natal chart that make you unique, so that when you read this book, remember that talking about a Virgo or a Scorpio can only be a beginning to knowing someone, the larger continents and oceans on their own psychological globe. These reactions and characteristics are not the only way a person will respond to situations. But Sun signs give guidance to the general way we feel, love and interact.

Unless your lover's Sun sign is severely afflicted, or has another more prominent sign in the natal chart, then he or she should be fairly consistent with the Sun sign image, though you may not recognise it instantly.

The sign rising over the horizon at the moment of birth has an equally powerful bearing on our psychological make-up. However, finding this out requires exact and detailed calculations, including certainty of time of birth. That is why our Sun sign is our primary pin-pointer on the map. You may not at first glance recognise yourself, because often your Sun sign reveals characteristics to which you don't want to admit!

As La Rochefoucauld put it so succinctly, 'Not all those who know their minds, know their hearts as well.'

The 12 Signs as Lovers and Partners

THE ARIES MAN

Aries is traditionally the first sign of the zodiac and that means that an Aries man comes first in everything. The Arien lover is bold, demanding, impulsive, and most certainly self-centred, and yet he will take risks in his relationships and in love. Because he cannot stand any kind of restriction to his freedom, you're more likely to find him hanging around motor races, rallies, outdoor activities rather than cutting cigar ends down the local pub. He's looking for adventure and, for the egotistic Ram, love-affairs are as much a challenge to him as hang-gliding.

One of the things that make him an exciting lover is his need to take chances. Romance to this impetuous man involves dragging you round the Himalayas at breathtaking speed and expecting you to eat vindaloo for lunch and dinner when you get back to the local Indian restaurant. He expects weekends in the camper in freezing winter with only each other to keep you warm! He needs a woman with guts both spirited and physically non-combustible to keep up with his vigorous lifestyle.

The arrogant Ram can fall in love easily, and impulsively, and if he genuinely believes that you are the answer to his dreams, he won't hesitate to become deeply involved. His sexual magnetism is tremendous, and he is so aware of his ability to attract women that he sometimes assumes that no one will reject him. This kind of arrogance can lead him into trouble, but his honest, no-nonsense approach always gets him back on top and he doesn't suffer from self-pity, ever.

What you must remember is that Arien hotheads are jealous Fire signs. It's quite all right for him to chat to other women, or even play a touch of harmless flirting, but for you to attempt even a smile at that charming colleague of his across the pub is fatal. In a crowded room you'll know the Aries man because he's the one with the self-confidence and the smile of a dare-devil lover. He might hastily introduce himself, arrogance and impulse working overtime to meet his challenger head-on. But if you crash, watch out for his honest vent to his feelings. It takes a lot to rile an Aries but, if you don't play fair and true, he won't let you forget it.

If you want a permanent relationship with him and can keep up with his energetic sex life you will be rewarded. But never forget that the Ram's egotism governs his need to satisfy himself first, and you second. But if you both can get over his self-centred approach to love and sex, for really he's always searching for an ideal, there is a lot of warmth and honest love waiting in his heart.

THE ARIES WOMAN

The Aries woman usually will want to be the boss in everything, including her love life. Because she is a Cardinal Fire sign, she knows intuitively what she wants. Some Aries girls will come straight to the point and pick you up, if you don't make the first move! Like her male equivalent, an Aries girl has great sexual magnetism, and if you're strong enough to take her on, you'll realise why her hot-headed vanity works.

Undoubtedly she will want to take over your whole life if

you fall in with her hard-headed approach to relationships. She will always be ambitious for you, and for where she comes in your life. She is number one, and you will always be number two. If you can bear her egotistic pride then she will be the most loving and passionate partner, but she needs commitment, and she needs to be the centre of your world, or she'll dump you.

Another important consideration is that exclusivity is her *raison d'être*. And that will mean you. Once she's let you into the secret art of ram-shearing then she can get incredibly jealous if you stray out of the sheep pen. She may be a passionate lover, but that passion doesn't make her liberal about free love.

The Ram girl likes men to be young in outlook and appearance. If you've got the energy to go hang-gliding before lunch then you'll be her friend for life. But if you've got a gut hanging out over your trousers and would rather sit in front of the TV with a can of lager, forget having any relationship with her. She needs an energetic man both as a friend, to make impulsive trips and exciting journeys, but also in bed. There is a fire burning in her soul which doesn't need to be put out, it just needs rekindling from time to time. The adventure in her head and the energy in her blood keep her restlessly searching for the next impulsive trip on love. Love is beautiful if she can be the boss, and she can take control, but give her back as much as she puts into a relationship and you'll stay her adventure for life.

THE TAURUS MAN

The natural inclination of Mr Bull at dawn is to force himself out of the bed he cherishes so much. But that's the only bit of forcing he'll do, particularly in any relationship. If he wants you then *you* have to be the one to chase him, but the move will be welcomed. A Taurean male won't actually make many advances and stubbornly waits for those who are worthy of his incredible sensual attention to come running.

For all this laid-back man-appeal it may appear that sex means little to him. But actually that's the catch. The Taurean male's quite seething sexuality, once unleashed on an unsuspecting female who decides to consider him as her partner, can be quite overtly bestial.

He thinks as highly of his body as he does of the next meal or the next bath. The Bull loves the pleasures and luxuries of life and is essentially an implacable part of the earth, intensely sensual, and dependable. He is an Earth sign whose energy and sexual drive originates from all that natural organic goodness that ironically he rarely eats.

There's actually something quite elusive about Taureans. You can never quite fathom out where they've come from, or really exactly where they are going to, probably because they really have no idea, nor care about it themselves. This is why it can take a long time to form a deep relationship with a Bull. If you do get past the horns, this affair could be for life. The placid Bull needs gentle handling, both emotionally and sexually. The trouble is that Mr Bull is often very blind to his own compatibility ratings. He is lured by, and hopelessly attracted to, Fire and Air signs. The Taurean man often gets tangled up with the Airy intellect or impulsive brainstorming of these very opposite types from him. He just can't keep up with the mind-bending improvisation that these signs so naturally use to charm their way through life.

The Taurus man is warm-hearted and affectionate, and he is intensely passionate. But he is a lover of the pleasures of life, a hedonist in every self-indulgence, and every luxury. Sex is a good, basic pleasure which he enjoys as part of a deep and erotic relationship. If after a heavy night of wining and dining he prefers to sleep off the last glass of brandy rather than spend the night with you, it's not that he's selfish, just that he forgot you for a while. After all, there are other sensual things in his life apart from sex, had you forgotten that?

THE TAURUS WOMAN

It's hard to imagine the placid, reliable, earth mother as a hard-edged Bull, but there is a side to her which might have been overlooked! A Taurean female takes a long time to decide if you are worthy of her passion, yet she has the power and the guts actually to initiate the first move in a relationship and should never be underestimated. A bossy girl needs careful handling, and because she is strong-minded and loyal she needs first-class devotion in return.

The Bull lady bears little resemblance to bovine sexuality except for an occasional grumbling temper and a geyser of bubbling anger when she gets overheated by resentment. Pouts grow on a female Taurean's lips very easily. Jealousy is uncommon, but possessiveness is. Her placid, controlled approach to your relationship is her self-protection, her magic eye. She has to impress and be impressed, which is why she often gets tangled up with men with a big cheque book. She likes the sound of champagne corks flying and the permanence of marriage.

Sensuality is the Taurean girl's be-all and end-all. It could be the summer rain pattering on your back as you kiss beneath an umbrella, or making love in the pine forest or beside the babbling stream. She's a creature of the outdoors, of closeness to nature and filling her senses with tastes, sounds and touch.

Venus in cowhide will be delighted equally whether she's having sex, floating in a silky warm ocean, eating pizzas at three in the morning, or cooking you both a cordon bleu breakfast in a tent. Sex is not to be taken lightly and she can get quite prudish with women who are apparent flirts or downright promiscuous. Convinced that a good emotional and sexual relationship is the answer to fulfilment, she might well confide her Mother Earth instincts to you one warm night.

The awkward and niggling little word 'possession' might create a spot of tension but, if you're willing to be a mate for life, or at least more permanent than the fading perfume on her skin, you will have to take sex and love as seriously as she does. If you can offer her honesty and maybe a sound financial future, a superb champagne dinner or a night listening to the owls in the woods, then she will be impressed enough to let you through her tough, resilient Bull-skin.

This girl needs both erotic and sensual communication, a man who can give her a down-to-earth lifestyle and a really warm heart. But make sure you've got the stamina and nerve to accept her blatant honesty if she decides to reject you!

THE GEMINI MAN

The highly versatile, spontaneous and amusing Gemini man is always ready for any mental and sexual challenge. He lives in the air, rather than flat-footed on the ground. Passion and sensuality are a rarity in his love life, for he is the catalyst of communication. The will o' the wisp is inquisitive, and like a child he will want to play games, will move through your life like a shooting star, and never make promises about tomorrow. He is privileged with a youthful appearance and a youthful approach to life. But emotionally, Gemini men rarely let you into their space, in fact they can often seem very cold, in the air, out of their heads and hardly ever in their hearts.

The second problem with which you have to wrestle is that there are always at least two personalities to cope with in one guise. This can be quite alarming when you wake up in the morning with a total stranger, not the man you thought you spent the night with! The seductive and alluring man of the late evening can turn into the clown at breakfast, and never be prepared to stay for lunch. The cherub-like Botticelli twins are actually not so much twins as a couple of conmen, both trying to outwit the other. Because of the mental struggle of trying to figure out his own identity, a Gemini male needs variety and change in his life. This means that he is often promiscuous, often marries at least twice and always wants two of everything. He has this uncanny ability and agility to be all types of lovers imaginable because role-playing stops him from ever being truly himself. And actually he really doesn't know who he is himself.

The double-lover enjoys the company and friendship of females just as much as any intimate physical relationship. Sexually he is the least chauvinistic of the star signs, and would rather spend the evening discussing the world and sipping champagne with you than be down the pub with the boys. He prefers to move on, to change partners, to try out new experiences, whatever forecast is in the wind, and to leave the fog of commitment and emotion far behind him.

If you can give him fun and variety he might even hang around to breathe your kind of fresh air. The Gemini man is often likened to Peter Pan, but if you ask any girl who's been involved with the Twins, she'll say, 'Sure, he reminded me of Peter Pan; but wasn't he like all those lost boys too?'.

THE GEMINI WOMAN

The female twins sparkle at parties, vibrating among other women who would rather keep cool and mysterious and watch this flirting charmer draw men to her like junkies to a fix. That's why a distortion of the facts has arisen and Miss Gemini has been dubbed two-faced in love, and a hypocrite in bed. So it's about time the true nature of this multi-faceted woman was revealed!

They seek out and need constant change in both their social lives and their love lives, not to mention their careers and their home life. Miss Fickle can jump headlong from the trivial to the profound in a split second because she's more interested in actual cleverness than the truth. She may have two or more faces, but they are all *genuine* in her own eyes, and in her own pretty head. Gemini girls are adept at role-playing, from switching from heaven to earth. Give them a character, a *femme fatale*, an innocent virgin, a career woman, you name it, they can play it. If you can keep up with their flighty, pacey, restless way of life, then you'll have more than one woman to keep you company at bedtime.

Apart from the thousand faces that Gemini women possess they are also known to be incredible flirts. It's not so much that she's particularly infatuated with you, it's more likely that she wants to play the game, drink her way through a bottle of champagne and then go home to sleep off the mental exhaustion of it all. She needs a lot of sleep, but a Gemini woman is more likely than any other sign to prefer to sit up all night discussing the latest philosophy, or the latest painting in your collection, or the books on your shelf.

She makes vague attachments, and loves socialising, but very rarely makes deep friendships, particularly with her own sex. Miss Fickle prefers the company of men to women and would rather be one of the boys at the office.

Gregarious girls meet a lot of blokes, so Gemini woman will be well surrounded by a choice selection. But remember, she's attracted to appearances rather than to depth of emotions. She is capable of persuading herself you're the love of her life. Being in love is easy if you talk yourself into it. Why, then, you can talk yourself out of it again when it takes your fancy, or another man does! (By the way, a Gemini girl's heart is a pretty cold place to penetrate, but if you ever get through the surface with your ice-pick at least you take pleasure in knowing that you will be remembered in her heart for being the only man that ever made it!)

The Jekyll girl often has affairs with younger men because she feels safer; commitment won't be spread across the bed with the Sunday papers at eleven in the morning after a night of hot passion. The marmalade men, the electric shavers and the city bods who need slippers and pipe won't attract her. She is capable of finding something fascinating and appealing in practically all men, but that doesn't mean it will last more than the second that it takes for her to change their mind, instantly! Enjoying sex isn't the answer to her dreams, only another dream can have that solution. And you can't stay her dream for ever – or can you?

THE CANCER MAN

The Cancerian man is home-loving, gentle and sincere. He responds deeply to life and to every change in emotion or feelings around him. His goodness far excels his weaker, depressive side which can get unbearable and drown an affair in melancholy. His moods can be touchy, he can be as snappy as an alligator and he takes everything too personally, fearing rejection. Yet on the surface he will play the extrovert, be flirtatious, the lunatic everyone loves at the all-night party.

A Crab man is overtly sentimental. He will take a long time to pluck up enough courage to phone you, until he is sure in his Crab-like way he can move in for love. Don't forget, Crabs move sideways, stay in their shells and guard themselves ferociously with giant claws.

He might seem mildly indifferent: playing guessing games about his true motives with you when he first takes you out to dinner.

He loves food, and if you offer him breakfast in bed he might just agree to scrambling the eggs himself. This man needs smothering with affection, and sexually can be languid and lazy when it suits him, especially once he feels secure in a relationship. Typical of Water signs, he feeds on gentle rhythms, quiet arousal and delicate love-making.

Don't ever mention your past boyfriends because he will see vivid mental movies about where you have been, and who you have been with. Cancerians are very possessive, and if you mention ex-partners, he will wallow in self-pity for days.

Don't ever look at anyone once you're married. You are collected, part of his acquisitions and his very personal private collection.

Cancer men hide out in the dark corners of pubs, or at the edge of the in-crowd. If they use their extrovert shell to cover up their weaker personality they can be awkward to spot. Sometimes they hover in the wings, hiding from possible failure, appearing as confident and glib as any fire sign. But around the full moon you can usually spot them when they become touchy and moody, not at all like any Fire sign!

The Crab is easily flattered, and often gullible in the face of a strong protective, woman. He has a cheeky, little-boy-lost appeal that he takes to parties in his search for the perfect soul-mate, and he needs one desperately for all his apparent self-confidence and arrogant manner. It's misleading. Beneath that gregarious shell is a soft heart. There will only ever be one woman at a time for a Cancerian man – at least you can be assured of that.

THE CANCER WOMAN

When you meet the Cancer woman you will immediately know that you have met the most female of all females. The Yin is intense, explosive, warm and genuine, the genie of the zodiac, the sensitive soul, the Moon disabled by love and emotion. You have nothing to fear, except yourself, and the changeability of her deep and dark side. The dark side of the Moon waits for you. Do not disappoint her for the woman with whom you have just become infatuated is the past-mistress of love and romance.

Cancer ladies are easily flattered and at their worst are unstable. Preparation for a life of swaying moods, indistinct emotions and powerful sensitivity have adapted this dippy bird to seek attention and seek out sympathy from a nice guy, one she hopes will have a larger cheque book than her own.

She is protective, gentle, highly intuitive and reflective of others' moods. Yet like the Moon she sways, changing the light of the night from that pale ghostly shadowland to human and loony laughter. A bit touched, a bit sad, occasionally glad, Moon birds need close friends, domesticity and a strong, tender man to support them.

You can only get so close to a Moon bird. She has this intense fear of being opened up like a clam. The big problem for her is that if she doesn't open up then you might reject her like the bad mussels in the cooking pot that get tossed in the bin. Frankly, the Cancerian girl needs a permanent, stable relationship with someone who won't get twisted and confused every time she sulks or goes loopy in the Full Moon. You've been introduced to an apparently hard, tough, thick-skinned woman in the crowd. It really seems unlikely that someone so extrovert and resilient could be reduced to tears by a slight put-down. But she can! She's an extrovert/introvert, a manic depressive and a bundle of fun when she's on one of her highs. She can be downright rude and criticise everything about you from your haircut to your taste in underwear but she won't survive an in-depth dissection of her own deeper and often weaker character. Cancer women will never make the first move, because they sincerely cannot cope with rejection.

A word of warning. This lady can get her claws into you quicker and more deviously than any other Crab this side of the Moon. The claws of a Crab can grab you and, pincer- like, they'll clutch at your heart and possessively monopolise you, as she possesses her books, her kitchen memorabilia and her dog.

Her imagination sizzles in bed, like throwing water on fire. But she needs emotional and sensual fulfilment, a physical experience that will change as easily as her moods. Cancerian ladies don't take to athletic body-building, or get obsessed about their weight, but they will make or break the sexual traditions if it means pleasing the one man they really want to impress.

THE LEO MAN

The Leo man is known for his magnanimous nature and his warm and generous heart. But he is also a prowler, one of the more sexually active signs of the zodiac. Like Capricorn and Scorpio he is motivated by power. The subtle difference is that Leo assumes success in everything he does, particularly when it involves relationships and love. He can't bear the thought of rejection so he never even thinks about it. That's why he blazes his way through life, and that is how he wins.

For all his flash behaviour the tom-cat is actually in need of a lot of stroking. He falls in love easily, but it will often be subconsciously motivated by the desire to impress his companion. The Cat is a show-cat, wherever and whoever he is with. Leos have dramatic tastes, extrovert and extravagant desires, unnerving energy and yet he is so self-opinionated that he can be intolerably conceited and inflexible.

They need to be in the headlines and to draw attention to themselves, so the Leo lover will look for the sort of woman who can enhance his Mogul image and taste for hedonistic delights.

If you're good-looking, independent, can hold your own and be part of his show, then he'll fall in love with you on sight. The one thing you have to remember is that the golden boy, for all his showiness, is actually not very brave. He doesn't take risks like an Arien or Sagittarian, and he generally takes more care about who he gets involved with to avoid hurting his delicate pride. His emotions are fiery, but his judgment is cautious.

For long-term commitment, a Leo will be willing to take the risk only if he gets as much attention as he believes he deserves.

He will have mastered all the techniques of high performance love-making. That is something that he can really impress you with. But while you're enthralled by his energetic love and sexuality, remember that he likes to play the Tom-and-Jerry game. Mostly he prefers to be Tom, but even Tom needs a lot of affection and warmth, for all his boasting conceit. Cold, unresponsive girls can make him temporarily impotent and turn that organised high-flyer to anger; and that's when he can really leave a trail of charred hearts!

THE LEO WOMAN

The Cat woman is one of those girls who is always surrounded by men at social events. She will insist on being the centre of attention at all parties, which is one of the reasons she always organises them. The Leo girl also assumes she will be the nucleus and hotbed in any relationship and, for her, relationships need to be warm, affectionate and full of physical expressions of love. Bear-hugs, stroking her wild hair as if she is a pussy-cat are all gestures that show how she is adored. And she needs that very badly. This naturally vivacious, clever Cat finds men drawn to her like mosquitoes to blood.

This very sexual Cat can at times be overpowering and overdramatic, but her magnetic personality always catches the limelight.

Leo was born to lead, and not to follow. If you are strong

enough to challenge her, then she may play the role of a sweet innocent for a while. But if she's not the starring role in your life then the loud, extravagant will of her ego will come hurtling out to confront you. And a Leo in full temper and voice is a pretty frightening Big Cat!

Her vanity irritates other women and attracts many men, and she can be arrogant and incredibly stubborn. She is self-opinionated, but she is also generous and compassionate, able to create the kind of atmosphere in the bedroom fit for the most sensual and seductive love-making imaginable!

If you can keep up with her energy and delight in passionate and exciting sex, then she might decide to make you a permanent fixture. The Cat woman will scratch for her independence, and won't sacrifice her career or freedom for many men. Although she will flirt her way through a boardroom of old fogeys to assure success in her career, you will have to trust her integrity.

Flatter her and she'll let you closer. Her vanity and her magnetic personality are, ironically, her weakness. But with respect and belief in a Leo woman you can be assured of a loyal and true partner. Never try to control her or play ego games. She needs a strong man who will pamper her; give her the world and in return she'll give you everything back. Attention-getting, and attention-seeking go together, so be prepared for the occasional mild flirtations when she's out at her business lunches, or career parties. If she weren't the star of the show someone else would be, and she really doesn't want anyone else to take that leading part away from her.

THE VIRGO MAN

If anyone could be more accurate, more perfect at time-keeping than a quartz watch, then it would have to be the Virgo man. He is the precision master, the careful and discriminating quiet one in the corner of the bar, who will drink exactly the same amount of alcohol every visit, and who knows precisely the health advantages of wine and the mortality rate of heavy drinkers. This neat and tidy man often pulls weights down the gym rather than girls, and worries about his digestion and whether he should be celibate.

The Virgo man finds warm, emotional relationships difficult, and yet he seeks out quality and the perfect woman. He analyses sex and relationships with the meticulous interest of a stamp-collector. You see, Virgo men don't really need anyone else in their lives. They often panic about their lack of passion, and then devote an awful lot of time worrying about it. (Virgos are constantly fretting about life.) Mr Precision sometimes falls in love with the logic of a relationship, with the actual methodology of it all, but very rarely is deep and genuine emotion involved.

Virgo men have this thing about purity. Not that they are chaste and virginal, but they will search for the purist form of experience and will often sublimate passion for neutrality. This is why if you're not near perfect in his eyes you'll be rejected before he even attempts to test you out. Sex can be a pure and impeccable experience for a Virgo with a girl in mint condition and the right motivation. But is there any life in his soul, any passion or warmth in that apparent cold and solitary physique?

He is very attractive to women because he appears to be a challenge. If you get past that cold shoulder there might just be a sensual, sensational warm heart. He has a heart, but it's as invulnerable as his emotions. On the surface he is the perfect lover and can perform like Don Juan. He is the sexual technocrat of the zodiac. If you can put up with his dissection of your personality, if you like a distant lover and a punctual friend, a lover who is dextrous but unemotional, he might make one of the better permanent relationships. But he compartmentalises life: the past stays the past, the future the future. He carries little sentimental or emotional baggage with him. It's tidier, isn't it?

If you finally get through the cold earth that buries this

man you'll find a faithful lover. He's not exactly a bundle of laughs, but the strong silent type who once he's found his perfect partner will never, ever look at another woman again.

THE VIRGO WOMAN

The Virgo girl is quiet, self-aware and keeps her eyes firmly pinned on anything that might remotely interfere with her calculated plans for life. This includes her personal relationships which are as critically analysed and subjected to meticulous scrutiny as if she were conducting a witch hunt or a scientific experiment.

Miss Virgo is not only critical of herself, she is acutely critical of others. She nit-picks rather than knits, and can really infuriate you with her constant reminder that you have a speck of dandruff, or your tie is wonky. She believes that she knows best, and this confident mental sharpness affects all her personal and sexual relationships.

She expects tidiness and perfection around her which includes an organised pristine relationship with her ideal man. The Virgo girl can lack real human warmth at her worst and, because she is such a worrier, even sex can become a chore, and your performance tainted with imaginary faults.

But a Virgo girl loves romance: the first innocent kiss or the love-letters scribbled from a stranger. She can become infatuated with someone over the phone, or by the pure physical beauty in a man. She loves sentiment and delicate love-making. An Interflora sign will make her weep and she's nuts about soppy films, as long as no one is with her when she watches them. If you are too dominant a partner she can become frigid just to suit herself. Coldness is natural to her.

Perfection is wasted on talentless men and she will often be fatally attracted to opposite dreamy types, escapist musicians and artists who, although they fulfil her romantic fantasy, lead her to find fault with every work of art or creation they perform. The Virgo girl is dedicated to pursuing happiness, and her strength is to be able to be both obsessively practical and ridiculously romantic, because love is the purist form of analysis.

Sex will be a delight to her if you keep it light and emotionless, but don't ever be late for a date, or her time-keeping will start clocking you in and out of her bed. She'll never be unfaithful, it's not in her nature. But if you can't enflame that spark of sexuality out of her ice-box she will quite coldly and mercilessly look for it elsewhere. The modest, clever and cautious Virgo girl will be the most affectionate and prudent partner if you can accept her perfectionism. She might decide you're her ideal and throw a party; but she'll stay in the kitchen and worry about the spilled punch. Someone has to haven't they?

THE LIBRA MAN

Libra is the go-between of the zodiac – the man who can be active or passive, will be laid-back, indecisive and fluctuate between love and sex in his head, easy-going, well mannered and everybody's friend. Doesn't that sound like the sort of man you would love to have around? Someone with wit and humour, who curves through life rather than angles through it? He is essentially a relaxed man who is fair and lovely about the world and naturally charming with every female he meets.

He needs harmony, beauty and idealistic truth in his life. For him, life has to fulfil dreams of romance, particularly when love and sex are involved. But this is where he gets confused. Not because he's a soppy sentimentalist, far from it, but because he thinks sex is love and love is sex. You just can't have one without the other, it wouldn't be fair.

This sociable man needs and demands a lot of friends of

both sexes. If you get involved with a Libra be prepared to tolerate all the other female friends he spoils. Some of them may even be ex-lovers that he hasn't quite decided whether to see again or not.

But there are times when a Libran won't be forced into making a decision at all and, when it comes to any conflict, emotional or physical, he would rather walk out than fight. The eternal problem for Librans is *not* making a decision. What bugs him is why he has to make a choice about commitment in his relationship, because essentially he hates to reject anything, and that mostly includes his freedom.

He wants the best of both worlds, if he can get it, and flirting his way through life enables him to meet many women, and maybe, just maybe, he'll find the girl of his dreams. He often gets led astray by strong, glamorous females. He can fall instantly in love, but he falls in love with the essence of the affair, rather than the girl. The face value of the romance is all that matters to him initially.

Like Gemini the Ping Pong man is attracted to the appearance of life, not any underlying spiritual meaning.

He's a romantic and a balloon-seller of ideals, releasing them on a windy day to see if they fly alone. He loves the romance of sex, the caresses, the body language, the first meetings. Sexually his head rules his body. His approach is one of airy, cloudless skies and often a languid, lazy love-making. But his soaring passion is an insubstantial mental process, and he often has trouble 'being there' with you.

This sexual egalitarian is a wonderful lover and romantic, but remember, he can fall out of love as easily as he fell into it!

THE LIBRA WOMAN

What if you meet a Libran woman surrounded by a group of adoring friends and she decided you were the most attractive, exciting man in the room? You invite her to dinner and she falls in love with your eyes and your hair and immediately and uncharacteristically accepts the date. An hour later the chances are she'll change her mind, or sweetly point out that actually she is with Tom, an old flame, and really she can't accept because they are already going down the pub that night. What if Tom got upset? And what if Tom really was the man of her life, the ideal she's searching for? And then what if she rejects your offer and you don't make another? This is the terrible dilemma for a Libran woman.

She is lovely, perfectly lovely. Attractive, gregarious, articulate, spirited and independent. A real woman but with a tough head and a strong heart. She's mentally alert and logical about life like any Air sign, but she really hates to reject anything, or anyone. And making decisions just means not having the best of both worlds, doesn't it?

Libran women have deliberately charming smiles which they can turn on when it suits them, to show how wonderfully feminine they can be. But the logical intensity of her mental gymnastics can be slightly off-putting if your intentions are of a deeper or more physical need.

She needs honesty, beauty and truth around her, no heavy emotion and no remorse. She'll cheer you up when you're down, brighten your life with her sparkling humour and will thoroughly enjoy sexual pleasure and hedonistic delights. Don't be a spoilsport or a worm, and if you can't find your way out of a paper bag then you're not her kind of man.

She'll love you for ever if you are her mental equal and her physical mirror image. But remember, this girl can be led astray by beauty and by the idea of love. Like her male counterpart, she can fall in love with the affair before she knows who you are. She'll listen to your opinions about politics, point out her own, then with equal fairness spout everyone else's point of view. That's why getting close to her heart can take a long time. She talks a lot, and she talks for everyone. Can you really find her beneath all those fair judgments?

THE SCORPIO MAN

Apart from a snake or a hypnotist, a Scorpio man has the best chance of fixing his penetrating eyes upon the one he loves or lusts and capturing her. No matter how hard you resist if he gets it in his head to seduce you, this man will hypnotise you before you've got back from the bar with your glass of white wine.

Like any insect, the Scorpio male has the ability to rattle and repel. You can meet him at the standard office party and find him offensive and unnerving, disagree with him about every subject under the sun, but he'll have you, and there's nothing you can do about it!

In Yoga, Kundalini is the serpent who lives at the base of our spine and is awakened upon sexual arousal. Any true Scorpio male's Kundalini is on permanent red-alert. To him sex and love are the whole meaning of life and the answer to every emotion. His attraction to women is motivated by his obsession for finding the truth, and often he falls prey to his own intentions by a touch too much promiscuity. The trouble is Scorpios actually need long-term and stable relationships. But the man is dangerous if you are on his hit-list. He'll pursue you secretively at first. If you find you are the chosen one he can also take over your whole existence.

Sometimes Scorpio will adore you until he actually destroys love, and you, in his mind and soul. It's the regenerative process of the Pluto passion, so you might as well enjoy the attention and the ecstasy while you can before he kills the love he has created.

His jealousy is intense. He lives and breathes every emotion, and with it love. He'll surprise you with spicy and secret rendezvous. In bed he'll be the connoisseur of all things sexual and emotional. He will want sex to be a symbolic, esoteric experience that sometimes falls close to obsession. Sex is big business to him and he can justifiably prove it with his reputation of a discreet but highly dangerous lover. But he has incredibly high standards and you must be spotless, almost virginal. The Scorpio male wants all or nothing, and the longer your mystery is prolonged the more intense the turn-on he gets.

You have to be emotionally and mentally strong to have a relationship with this man. If you think you can handle him, can bear the shock when his eyes start to penetrate another victim's heart across the room, beware! This man is powerful. A boa constrictor takes a very long time to kill its prey – by gently squeezing the life out of it; until it can breathe no more.

THE SCORPIO WOMAN

The powerful seductress of the zodiac takes life seriously, too seriously at times. When she first sets eyes on you she will want to dominate you both physically and emotionally. Scorpio girls have an intuitive awareness of their sexual magnetism and, like sparks of static electricity, you will feel her presence in the room, whether you've met the haunting gaze of her eyes or not.

Watch out when she's about, for this dark, deeply motivated lady can play any charming role, any teasing subtle game that will make you think you are in control, not her.

If she could, the female snake would have been born a man, but as she has to bear the physical weakness of woman, she is more like the Medusa's head than one serpent, and more like a dozen Plutonian meteorites than a simple solitary moon.

For a Water sign she gives a pretty good impression of a Fiery one. Playing the *femme fatale* is easy for she creates subtle intrigue, the mystery and enigmatic power of a genie or a sorcerer. She can be hot and dominating one minute, then an emotional wreck the next. She'll hate voraciously and she'll love passionately. Whatever emotion she feels, she feels with intensity.

If she falls in love with you it will, for that moment, at least be for ever. Playing games with her is fatal, and if you start thinking the relationship should remain casual and lighthearted you might get a shock when she starts calling you on the phone in the middle of the night with tears, threats and demands.

Strength in a man is the Scorpio girl's weakness. The more independent, the more ambitious you are, the more she will love you. Sex and love are like a parasite and its host; without one you can't have the other. Remember, she takes her relationships very seriously and will sacrifice you for another if it means the total fulfilment of her soul.

Power is crucial to her existence and she won't be thwarted. Her strength of character is admirable, and her sexuality is so intense that it could take a lifetime really to know her. Secrets are big words for Scorpio girls, so make sure you have plenty, but keep her own mystery to yourself.

THE SAGITTARIUS MAN

The Archer is born altruistic, bold and voracious. It seems that he has the spirit and the morals of an Angel but watch out, the legendary bowman is more likely to have the soul of a gambler and the morals of a sexual extortionist. With unnerving blind faith and the optimism of Don Quixote this happy-go-lucky man wins his way through life and relationships like a trail of fiery stars. His honest and blunt admission for loving women make him the sort of guy that other men hate and women adore. It's not the egotistic vanity of an Aries, nor the power-driven motivation of a Leo; this Fire sign is genuinely convinced that this is the way things are. He can't help it if he was born beautiful, can he?

He's honest and open about himself, doesn't pretend to be something that he's not, and certainly lets you know if he's had enough of your company. He flirts easily, is really everybody's friend and is lighthearted and easy about life and women.

No strings and no commitments make this man's sense of freedom and need for a blank cheque in personal relationships sacrosanct.

Often the Archer looks for adventure, sexual or otherwise, as long as he can maintain his buccaneering spirit. That is why Sagittarians often resort to casual relationships to make sure there is nothing to stop their capricious wanderings. Meeting challenges head-on is the way the Archer travels through life and love. He responds to the thrill of the chase, of a woman who is hard to pick up. But he is idealistic and if you live up to his high standards he has the uncanny ability to know exactly how things are going to work out with you. If the Archer actually agrees to make an arrangement to meet you the following week and the stars are in his eyes as well as yours, you might think you had instigated the wonderful moment. But Sagittarians have this knack of making you think big, and sharing their expansive nature.

Like the other Fire signs, Sagittarians need outdoor activities and an extrovert lifestyle. If you can keep up with his active and quite fast-paced life he might consider you to be the pal he's looking for. Sex isn't everything to a Sagittarian, he needs someone to play mental and physical games too. He needs an inventive sex life, and his moods can range from passionate and fiery to warm and playful. Sex is fun, not a deep emotional experience.

So don't ever get soppy about him, he really doesn't like the kind of woman who hangs around like a lost doll, or who hasn't a life of her own. The Archer needs someone who is never possessive and rarely jealous, though on occasions he can be.

Watch out for the hailstones though, the Sagittarian can flash in and out of your life like a magnetic storm to avoid those rainclouds of commitment. But if he's convinced you're as free and easy, as unemotional and as unpossessive as he is, then maybe he'll forget about his unreliable and irresponsible attitude to life, and settle for permanent free love. That paradox is what he really wants.

THE SAGITTARIUS WOMAN

The outspoken Archer woman will insist on letting you know if you don't match up to her ideal, and she'll also pull your ideas apart with frank and brutal honesty which, to the uninitiated, can be a cultural shock. She lives independently and is always happier if her freedom isn't curtailed. Her honesty is genuine but it can sometimes cut through your heart like a butter knife, particularly as she's one of the most vivacious, amusing and popular females.

She prefers the company of men in any social setting and openly flirts in a rather innocent and childlike way. Like her Geminian opposite sign, she has no need for emotional depth to her relationships and prefers the surface attractions, the moles and wrinkles of appearances, rather than the viscera of human emotion. Friendship and companionship are more important than close emotional ties, and often platonic relationships with men and keeping friendly with ex-lovers is the easiest way to maintain her freedom and ensure an easy-going existence.

She can be so frank, that discussing her ex-boyfriends' intimate inclinations can sound like boasting to your ear, when she was only just letting you know how absurd she finds the whole sexual game. She doesn't mean to hurt anyone, never means to upset or put down a friend, and will end up confused and embarrassed by her own big mouth.

But an Archer girl's optimism spreads through her life and into her partner's with the ease of ripe brie. To be so confident, to be so sure that a relationship will work as long as she has her freedom, is a bonus to any partnership.

Communicating inner emotions and deeper tensions is not part of her vocabulary and that's why she often confuses love with casual friendship. Sex is also not to be confused with love, and she can have a strong physical relationship with a man and just be good friends. Being a pal is easier, doesn't lead to commitments, to arrangements, and traps like that big word 'love' always seems to do. If she's kept you up all night at a dinner-party, played the life and soul, flirted with your dad, and hardly noticed your jealousy, don't expect her to apologise. Her mind is set, and her morals are high, but she does like to have fun, her own way. If you want her to do anything, always ask nicely, never order her or tell her. She won't be bossed, in public or in private, or in bed.

Don't trap this incurable romantic. Don't question her, and you'll find her free love is all for you!

THE CAPRICORN MAN

The Capricorn male is often likened to that goaty god, Pan. On the surface Pan may be a dour, apparently bloody-minded hard-liner, but somewhere underneath it all you might find some true warmth and a consistently easy-going nature.

Capricorns are often conventional and rarely let themselves slip into any gear other than the one they have selected. In relationships with women they need to be in control. Even a power-mad Pan's chaos is controlled. In the wild abandon of infatuation his feelings and emotions are held from the precipice of freedom. He will be in charge of his destiny and yours, if you so much as show any inkling of desire for him.

He admires women who can coax him out of his stuffy Goat ways. But he also likes women who are ambitious for him too. Can this bedrock of society really rock the sexual and emotional bed? If he never deviates from his own tethering circle, will he ever have fun? A few women can release him from his rope of cold love. His inner nature often mellows as he ages, and oddly enough the paradox of this man is that as he gets older and more conventional he will also let go of any sexual inhibitions and allow spontaneous 'feelings' to enter his heart.

Pan often gets involved with women just for financial or career advancement. You'll often meet rich and successful females who have been taken advantage of by a Goat. Some of them have the man tethered on the dry arid plain of a monotonous marriage, but most of these Goats are already up there at the top of the mountain. The funny thing is that a Capricorn can digest all the flack you might throw at him for using you. A Goat's stomach speaks for itself!

The Capricorn man is shatterproof and biodegradable. Once he's decided you're the partner for his tenacious way of life, then he'll want to run you as smoothly as his business.

He can seem cold and passionless, restrained and indelicate in sexual communication. He is awfully possessive and it's very hard to change his opinions. But the taciturn Goat has a dry and witty sense of humour and there's always that twinge of inner warmth to draw out. He's not dull, but his approach to sex can be as disciplined and as ambitious as his approach to work. There is a closet romantic in his heart trying desperately to get out, and he needs a wise woman to open the door for him. As long as your relationship is within the boundaries of his own white lines, and he is in control, you'll find the most loyal and reliable partner behind those wardrobe doors.

THE CAPRICORN WOMAN

Don't ever expect a romantic encounter with this woman to last very long. She'll have all those graceful, feminine wiles, make all those suggestive noises about a full-scale affair, but the kissing and the innuendos and the candlelit dinners will last only as long as she wants them to. And that is often shorter than you'd imagined!

The Goat lady is always ambitious and she knows what she wants. If she wants you, she'll look beyond the romantic aspect of love for something more stable, more gutsy and more to do with a business arrangement than an emotional one.

She is often power-mad, whether it's in the office, or in a relationship. There's no point floundering around in bed making wild romantic promises, and sharing ideals when you can go for the real thing. A commitment, a permanent relationship. She doesn't relax in love easily and has a cool approach to sex and emotions. But if you give this Goat the lead she can be intensely passionate and will gradually lose her shyness once she's known you a long time. She has to control the affair her own way, but don't let her fool you into thinking her calm and bossy approach is the only backbone to her heart and her head. Her feathers are easily ruffled and, although she doesn't live in the twilight zone of feelings, she can get jealous and brood quite easily, and sulk if she feels slighted or betrayed.

She needs to know exactly where she's going in life and with you. Self-imposed discipline makes her sometimes pessimistic and will convince her that love is as shallow as your first kiss in the back of the black cab. Capricorn girls find intimate relationships difficult to handle unless they are really in charge, and that's why they make excellent partners or wives, but not very wonderful lovers.

The Goat lady needs her home and her mountain to climb. If she is sure you are worth pursuing she'll also ensure that she is ambitious for you too. A lot of Capricorn ladies are the true reason behind a man's career success! If you can let her take the lead through the chaos of emotion, not burden her with demanding encounters and weak-willed indecision, then she'll stay at the top of the one mountain she yearns to climb with you, called love.

THE AQUARIUS MAN

You have to remember that the space-age man is an unconventional and eccentric freedom lover, and yet wants to be everyone's friend and stick to his own quite rigid lifestyle. Aquarian men set out to find as many friends as they possibly can, rather than worry about love and sex. Love and sex are valid, and part of life, but they aren't the be-all of existence for this fixed Air sign. As long as the Water-Bearer sees change and progress in others, or in the world around him, then he is blissfully happy. He does not particularly pursue or encourage it in himself.

Our Uranus man is an out-of-space man. He's an oddball, a weirdo, often the man you meet at the office disco who doesn't drink and doesn't dance but smokes a pipe and looks like an anarchist. He might also be that man on the commuter train you see every morning who gazes at you with alien eyes and has an aloof and rather cold appearance. He's actually silently working you out, because Aquarians, like Frankenstein, enjoy scientific investigation of the human psyche!

His feelings about women can be as cranky as his habits, but there is one thing he will always do first before he makes any move to attempt a relationship: convince himself that you are strong enough to cope with his inquisitive and probing mind.

He feels it's his right to know everything about the woman of his choice, and the deeper the mystery you stir, the longer you remain an enigma, the more likely he'll want to nose-dive into your secrets. So make sure your game of 'catch me when you can' involves a worthwhile solution!

The secret of the universe, your sexual appetite, you name it, the Aquarian will unravel the truth to expose the answers. Sex is no less, no more, important than any other facet of his active life, and if you're happy to consider sex and love as part of your life too, then you'll stand a better chance of a long-term relationship with this man and all his friends.

Love is impersonal to an Aquarian. He takes it and hands it round with the same degree of feeling (and that's an awfully hard word for him to say) to everyone. Don't ever think that you are special. You can be part of his life, but never to the exclusion of others. Being friends is more important than being lovers. This is how he will choose a soul-mate: sex comes second to this Air sign who lives in his head and rarely in his heart.

He enjoys sex but as for other Air signs it's fun, a mental experience, not emotional, and definitely not soppy. Aquarius is an abstract lover who will blow cold rather than hot. He'll persist until he strips the outer bark of your personality like an icy wind bares the most beautiful and toughest trees. If you're still in one piece and agree to be his pal, that is what counts. Who needs lovers, when you can have a good and permanent friend?

THE AQUARIUS WOMAN

Possessions and possessiveness are not something an Aquarian woman will even consider in her emotional or sexual relationships, particularly from her partner. Her unpredictable and unconventional approach to life is formulated from a stubborn need to be awkward for the sake of it.

She needs mental rapport, companionship, and above all, friendship with a man: someone she can talk to all night and all day, who will stand by her, be loyal and genuine and caring about humanity as well as about the individual long before she'll even consider him as a possible mate in bed or in the home. Aquarian women often live alone better than with a partner and spend a good deal of their lives independently succeeding in careers rather than in motherhood.

The Uranian girl's emotional detachment keeps her free from forming too intense and personal relationships. It gives her an open lifestyle, the chance to encounter as many friends as she possibly can. If you can be her friend and not attempt to own her or try to change her and accept that you have to share her with the world as she shares you with the world, then you may have found a soul-mate. Her apparent lack of passion can be frustrating, but her loyalty is impeccable and her stability is supportive.

Passion implies commitment and intensity, and to an Aquarian girl both are abhorrent. She enjoys sex and physical contact as a pleasurable and warm activity between friends, but she won't ever let you get soppy or slushy. If you do she'll think you're weak and pathetic, and she needs a tower of strength in her bed, not a fragile sandcastle. She can take sex, or leave it.

The essence of an Aquarian girl's love is based on her need to force herself to be different, to be an eccentric. She will, of course, have delved into your mind, wriggled out your intentions, and scanned you with an emotional barium meal to check out if you're worthy of closer inspection. But if friendship isn't in your heart, then love and sex won't be in hers.

THE PISCES MAN

If you've ever gone fishing out at sea, on the glimmering darkling patches of the ocean where the water is black and the bottom of the sea runs deeper than the height of the tallest mountain, then you'll know exactly what a Pisces man is like to catch. Often you have to climb into that diving bell, and take a powerful torch to locate him. Sometimes he'll emerge only to escape from life into fiction and fantasy. He'll often prefer to drown in anything, as long as it's drowning.

Fish men are charmingly romantic and awfully attractive because they are such dreamers; a very different challenge from the passion of Fire signs, the mental agility and lightness of Air or the solid practicality and sensuality of Earth men.

Impressionable to the point of being blotting pads, they will see only what they want to see and cloud their incredible intuitive and psychic senses with careless indecision. Mr Denizen-of-the-Deep lives in a partial eclipse of life no matter what love-encounters throw at him. He is easily led astray by alcohol and women. The Fish will escape into shadowland and pretty dreams, rather than face the mundane reality of life. If he fails in a relationship it's simple: he retreats. For someone who is actually quite gregarious he drifts through life as the zodiacal mop, absorbing and sensing your changing moods.

The Fish men are drawn to very beautiful and very female women. They are easily besotted by physical beauty. Being in love is a good escape from real life, whether it's with a beautiful day, a beautiful drink, or beautiful women. You can lead a Piscean astray more easily than you can get a dog to eat a bag of crisps, and you can get him into an intimate sexual relationship faster than a black-cab meter spends your money.

Sexually he is uniquely gifted. He doesn't need words or books, passion and emotion flow easily and love grows quickly in his deep cave of feelings. But Piscean men are often too far away in their own fantasy, and if you're not open with him you'll get left behind on the shore while he's diving back down into the deepest part of the ocean for the water spirits.

This half-man, half-fish is only ever half-seen. If you are prepared to embark on a sea voyage with him, make sure you've got the sea-legs to follow him to the deepest part of the ocean when he leaves you for his own lonely ecstasy.

THE PISCES WOMAN

The mermaid is half-fish, half-girl, and the Pisces girl is half-way between reality and a dreamworld, far from any logical or mental plane, in a world of intuition and feelings. She is usually poised, beautiful, and compassionate. Love and caring is genuinely felt, and she is kind and uniquely sensitive to others around her. She is the girl who sells sea-shells on the sea-shore, a poetry of emotional fluidity.

Of course this kind of feminine mystique attracts men easily, so she is usually surrounded by a choice of the best fish in the sea. There are many Piscean women who have been badly hurt by rushing headlong into romantic involvements without a thought because they really do not think. The Mermaid suffers intensely from emotional pain, and bitterness can turn her fishy scales to higher melancholy octaves. She can be led astray by the temptation of romance, or by the masks of drugs or alcohol to hide from her own passionate feelings. The Mermaid is deep to find. Like diving for oyster pearls, she will be hidden, unfathomable, and never in shallow water. Her elusive nature is vague and sometimes dithery, and she will always be moving somewhere and never be sure where it is she should be going.

Love is a touch-down, a grounding from reality and she'll fall into it as easily as Alice fell down the rabbit hole. In love she gets carried away by emotion and the prevailing moods of her lover can channel her through the murkiest waters and the shimmering waves like driftwood. Yet sometimes the physical intensity of her sexuality will produce emotional conflicts within herself and she will begin to see the man she thought she loved as just another shell on her lovely sea-shore. She is like the tide that washes across the empty bay, surfing back the shells to find the one that glistens in the sun, rather than the ones that turn to sand. She needs to belong to the sea of love, and to one man, and that man must be strong and protective, and mostly understanding.

The Mermaid often falls for weak, nebulous and gifted characters, a lover who makes love and feels as deeply as she. But together they will drown each other. The tide that carries her on to a better shore is the man who turns up the oyster bed and finds the real pearls inside.

The 12 Signs as Friends

ARIES

The Aries friend is rather like a meteorite landing in your life. Full of energy and enthusiasm for your friendship one day, the next deserting you for another planet, leaving you feeling deserted. Ariens can make and break friendships faster than any other sign. They hate being dependent on anyone and, on the whole, would rather have many acquaintances than close pals. Ariens of both sexes enjoy the companionship of men, and the rough and tumble of fairly lively and noisy gatherings, but they can be quite happy with their own company. They find it difficult to keep platonic relationships with the other sex and are not known for their reliability as friends. They would rather ensure they are the centre of attention so, if others are prepared to tag along with them, they may just be pally while the going is good!

TAURUS

Bulls of both sexes make warm and considerate friends. They need close, intimate friends rather than loose and casual ones and prefer the company of individual pals to social gatherings. They are always generous and would prefer you borrow from them, rather than owe you any favour, yet they are genuinely concerned for your welfare. They need a lot of affection and tactile communication, bear-hugs and cheek-kissing, rather than just a nod, both from friends of their own sex and platonic friends of the other. They like to feel comfortable and will make great efforts to make you always feel at home in their own nests. If you ever need to phone for help, a Taurean is just the sort of person to get you out of trouble, without getting het up, but they may take their time getting there!

GEMINI

Gemini loves a varied and lively social life. Not very reliable when you make arrangements for outings, they are not very fond of very intimate, close friendships. They prefer a wide circle of acquaintants to the serious one-to-one friend. However, they are so adaptable that they will make friends very quickly, chatter about the world and generally enjoy themselves. They can be inconsistent, and also gossips in big circles, so as a close and trusted friend they are not really reliable. Both sexes like platonic friendships, and you often find they have more true friends of the opposite sex than they do of their own. Very gregarious, but not very loyal, they also like to feel they can leave when they want to, rather than have any restrictions to adhere to. They need friends who enjoy intellectual pursuits rather than the great outdoors. But they are adaptable, and will try anything new, for the sake of novelty.

CANCER

Crabs take a long time to make friends and therefore prefer to make firm relationships with people they can trust and have known for a long time. They don't enjoy big gatherings, and rooms full of people they don't know, but will enjoy socialising if it's among small groups of similar-minded people. Can be surprisingly obsessive about maintaining a close friendship and need to feel they can rely on someone to talk through all their own fears and woes. Cancerians are generally cautious about lending money, or any of their possessions, and don't particularly like being asked about their finances. Although they insist on depending on their close friends, they are also easily hurt if let down by others and can take it very much to heart. But they are wonderful at helping in a crisis, and will never let you down.

LEO

The Lion likes to roar and be the centre of attention in any social gathering. They make friends easily with both sexes and will often have a very wide circle of friends to amuse their ego-orientated heads. Leos make good friends and are more reliable than the other Fire signs. They are intensely loyal and will stick up for any one of their acquaintances if they get into trouble, or need supporting. Though not emotionally close to new friends, nor even to the old and trusted, they do need warmth and a fun-loving rapport to stay your pal for long. They are open-hearted and quite generous, but don't ever betray their trust or they can scratch back. Most Leos love socialising and parties, and are often the all-night party goers rather than the dinner party type.

VIRGO

They make difficult friends as they never quite get close enough to anyone, nor accept other people for what they are. They can be cold and judgmental, and also, once they think they know you, can seem quite critical. Yet they are good at socialising on a wider scale, and enjoy casual acquaintances and brief friendships so that they don't get caught up in emotion. On a wider scale they will be lively, fun to be with and enjoy intellectual and stimulating company. They are very cautious about who they invite into their house, and often prefer not to venture into other people's homes: it gets too warm! They like general chit-chat and would prefer to chat to friends in the pub and not make any commitments nor rely on others for anything. They are very single-minded but can be relied upon to organise any event or social gathering. Societies and clubs are their favourite way of keeping acquaintances around them and not getting tied down.

LIBRA

Libra is the most sociable and affable of signs. Librans love parties, social gatherings of all kinds and will always want to make friends with as many people as they possibly can. Librans are also quite a dab hand at keeping in touch with old friends, and they look on casual acquaintances with as much sympathy as they do someone they've known since childhood. Librans need a lot of company and don't enjoy the solitary life. As close friends they can be relied on, but they often have a habit of appearing interested in what you have to say when in fact their mind is somewhere else. They are not particularly deep, nor passionate about forming a close bond unless a friend is prepared to make an effort too. They love gossip and small talk, and don't enjoy lengthy philosophical discussions

SCORPIO

Scorpios are slow to make friends but, when they do, they make them for life. They aren't too fond of large gatherings, but may appear on the surface quite charming and outgoing. Underneath they are probably testing you out to see if you live up to their incredibly high standards! Most Scorpios need very close and intense friendships. Because it takes them so long to decide whether they have found a true and confidential pal, they often find that they lose friends quickly. They don't like to rely on anyone, but they will provide all the emotional support that anyone could need, and have admirable shoulders to cry on. Scorpios can usually and intuitively know if someone is a fair-weather friend but, once a bond is formed, they want it to be unbreakable and don't respond well to casual, light and inconsistent friendships.

SAGITTARIUS

Archers usually have a wide circle of friends, and prefer light and easy pals to any deep and meaningful ones! They move around so much that they are likely to make friends with strangers in the street. They are never suspicious, and never cautious and, if a friend turns out to be an enemy, they can shrug their shoulders and bear no malice, as they just move on to another one. Their open and freedom-loving approach to life makes them fairly unreliable friends to have. Although they can enjoy the company of their own sex and play light amusing games, they aren't good at any form of permanence. They don't like making arrangements and would prefer just to turn up when they feel like it. Both sexes like platonic relationships and feel more comfortable surrounded by many rather than a few.

CAPRICORN

Rather stuck in their ways, Capricorns are not good at making friends and not easy to make friends with! Both sexes prefer the company of men, and would rather form any relationship on a business arrangement than anything looser. They don't need a wide or varied social life and enjoy the company of a few friends who share the same ambitions or mental stimulation. Once they do form any strong friendship, they will try to keep it for life and do not take kindly to being let down. They are not particularly interested in giving or going to parties, and would rather talk in the boardroom or the pub where they feel safer in a neutral environment.

AQUARIUS

Aquarians are naturals at making friends; and keeping them. They love to have a wide variety and circle of friends, and will insist on maintaining endless platonic relationships to ensure that their altruism is genuinely felt. They are in need of mental rapport rather than any sporting or clubby basis for friendship. They are consistent and determined to supply any mental or emotional support they can handle. Although rather cold emotionally, they will always analyse friends, problems and crack the truth, rather than lead you into false promises. Although they prefer people with cranky or eccentric minds like their own, Aquarians enjoy the company of anyone who can stimulate them intellectually. They always say what they mean, and can often be awkward about your judgments. But they will never let you down in a crisis

PISCES

Pisceans are only slow to make friends as they are a little wary, for all their gregarious nature. They mix well in neutral surroundings and enjoy informal parties and gatherings where they can merge in with the crowd. They enjoy friends of both sexes and prefer to feel relaxed and non-committal rather than have pressures and obligations forced on them. They make wonderful friends when a rapport is established and are genuinely sympathetic, genuinely compassionate and always ready to help with any emotional comfort or support. They prefer a strong mental and intuitive friendship but can be too impressionable and soak up others' problems and bad habits rather than remaining independent of them. They often have a large circle of acquaintances and don't often have many close friends. Pisceans usually have one very old friend to rely on in times of trouble.

Some Famous Virgos

Martin Amis (25 August 1949)
Sean Connery (25 August 1930)
Mother Teresa (27 August 1910)
Sir Richard Attenborough (29 August 1923)
Ingrid Bergman (29 August 1915)
Van Morrison (31 August 1945)
Lily Tomlin (1 September 1939)
Raquel Welch (5 September 1940)
Britt Eckland (6 September 1943)
Gwen Watford (10 September 1927)
Barry Sheene (11 September 1950)
Ian Holm (12 September 1931)
John Smith (13 September 1938)
Jacqueline Bissett (13 September 1944)
Freddie Mercury (15 September 1946)
Agatha Christie (15 September 1890)
Greta Garbo (18 September 1905)
Twiggy (19 September 1949)
Michael Elphick (19 September 1946)
Sophia Loren (20 September 1934)

VIRGO COUPLES

𝄞

Business partners, past and present

The Hon. Charles Rolls (27 August 1877) and
Sir Frederick Henry Royce (Aries – 27 March 1863)
Dick Clement (5 September 1937) and
Ian La Frenais (Capricorn – 7 January 1937)
Peter Sellers (8 September 1925) and
Sir Harry Secombe (Virgo – 8 September 1921)

👥

Romantic couples, past and present

Prince Albert (26 August 1819) and
Queen Victoria (Gemini – 24 May 1819)
Lady Antonia Fraser (27 August 1932) and
Harold Pinter (Libra – 10 October 1930)
Lenny Henry (29 August 1958) and
Dawn French (Libra – 11 October 1957)
Pauline Collins (3 September 1940) and
John Alderton (Sagittarius – 27 November 1940)
Lauren Bacall (16 September 1924) and
Humphrey Bogart (Capricorn – 25 December 1899)
Anne Bancroft (17 September 1931) and
Mel Brooks (Cancer – 28 June 1927)
Jeremy Irons (19 September 1948) and
Sinead Cusack (Aquarius – 18 February 1948)
John Dankworth (20 September 1927) and
Cleo Laine (Scorpio – 28 October 1927)
Sophia Loren (20 September 1934) and
Carlo Ponti (Sagittarius – 11 December 1913)

Astro Meditations

**FOR YOU AND YOUR PARTNER
FOR 1994–1995.**

ARIES

Being first in everything is being part of everything. Use your energy and impulse creatively, spontaneously. Be you, but learn from gentleness. Fire is cosmic, don't burn others up, set them alight instead.

TAURUS

Hedonistic, jewels of sensuality. Pursue pleasures instead of waiting for them. Resentment builds on regrets. Take notice of energy, ground it if you must. Endurance is an art – respect it.

GEMINI

Seek change, but seek change within. Don't try to look deeper, you can't. The surface is coloured, is covered in shimmering. Let it be superficial, let your sexual love and lightness glide.

CANCER

Be a lunatic but face the truth that you have deeper emotions. Insecurity is instability. Sex and love can unite. Don't hide yourself from your truth – you are an introvert/extrovert. Light a candle to yourself.

LEO

Self-gratification. You love to impress, to make a noise, to have power. Power can be constructive, love and sexuality instructive. Flash warmth. Roar with pride rather than conceit.

VIRGO

Let go of the sex manual. Take a trip on surprise, on unpredictability, that is love. Stop worrying – be dippy. Perfect diffidence, it is as refreshing as your crisp mentality. Jog in bed, dissent.

LIBRA

Romance is born easily. Use charm explosively, no time for hesitation. Fall in love with love, but make it clear to yourself. Clarify romantic attraction and know it for what it is.

SCORPIO

Sentence only your obsessions. Keep others' mysteries as proof of emotions. You feel love as sexuality, as wholeness – the mystery and the answer to life. Fulfil your needs tenderly, administer with light.

SAGITTARIUS

You can expand, let others know. Give yourself freely, without blunt words. Wise to the world, wise eventually in love. Try loyalty, let go of promiscuity. Challenge sexual egotism with altruistic love.

CAPRICORN

Treat sex as an infant, nurture it. Grow with it, not against it. Try reaching out, try giving with the heart. There is no power in restriction, in restraint. Tie sex to love instead of to the bed.

AQUARIUS

Rebellion hurts others. Convention can work. Friendship is your heaven – let others come closer, let others conform if they must. Sex can be part of love, not a trap, it can be free.

PISCES

Ideals, half-seen, half-being. The stray are led astray more easily than the homed. The clouds can open with rainbows on the ocean. Take a deep-sea dive, communicate love instead of drowning.

Your at-a-glance chart showing
love trends for 1995

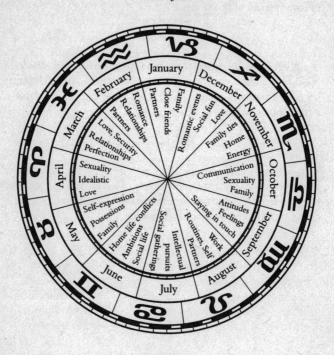

Virgo

The inner sections emphasise the important moods and
trends through each month of 1995 with regard to love,
friendship, partnership, sex.

Virgo

COMPATIBILITIES

VIRGO MAN – VIRGO WOMAN

For the precise and methodical Virgo to meet a girl so incredibly in tune and in time with his own lifestyle is probably the most enchanting, perfect moment he has ever experienced. Here is a girl who loves punctuality, admires his quiet and cool poise and is fascinated by his mental sharpness. Equally, when the Virgo girl climbs into bed the first time with the Virgo man, she is dumbfounded by the way he has mastered the art of love-making in the same manner as she's mastered the art of dissecting the turkey for Christmas. Liking the same method of living, and thinking the same in life is essentially a brilliant start for any relationship. But because they are so alike, they must learn to analyse their own faults which are clearly mirrored in each other.

Although these two are able to perfect their routine without interference, they actually stimulate one another's usually rigid mentality into becoming a more vibrant and lively one. In fact two Virgos chatter as much as two Geminis, the difference being Virgos are more analytical and critical; the Geminis, however, are actually communicating.

As both are uniquely gifted with tact, meticulous, and practical knowledge, they can support each other mentally and emotionally. They may get upset if they both worry about the same things.

Virgo men are likely to rise early and jog round the park, appear precisely at eight a.m., expecting the Virgo girl to have timed the eggs in the poacher. This kind of simple mental arithmetic causes few headaches. Virgos don't like scenes and emotions, and they don't like headaches. It might be the first sign of brain damage and they are awfully fond of their brains!

Although the Virgo man has perfected love-making for his own satisfaction, and the Virgo girl will at first be impressed by this, it's not because of the quality of his art and the pedantry of his style; in fact both are more fascinated by each other's minds than each other's bodies, and sexually they may both have a fairly cold relationship.

VIRGO MAN – LIBRA WOMAN

What these two have in common is that Libra rather admires Virgo's ability for self-discipline, and Virgo admires the Libran's fair play in everything. Admiration is a mutual stimulation for an otherwise fairly stark relationship. The Virgo Man is not particularly interested in the high life, in socialising, nor in charming the world and enjoying it. He also prefers predictability and would rather share his life with a placid, easy-going girl. This is how the Libran girl appears to be when he first meets her. He will fall in love easily with her bright, sparkling, Airy chatter and, mentally, she will provide him with a fascinating and constant strength of purpose. The Virgo doesn't want to be bossed, and he needs a companion rather than a lover. He doesn't like laziness, nor untidiness and, although he enjoys sex, he doesn't go wild about it. Now a Libran girl may find all this sharp, rather austere attitude a little mind-bending. She likes to have her brain well used, but she also loves to get out and about and enjoy herself. She may find the uncluttered existence of the Virgo rather cold and unwelcoming, his punctuality will irritate her and, as fair as she tries to be, she cannot quite justify in her head why she has to stay put, get up to catch the same train every day, and make decisions when she would rather avoid them.

If she does get as far as spending the night with him, it could initially seem a magical experience. She is not in need of passion and hot steaming beds and nor is he. But she does need warmth and affection and to feel really loved. The Virgo tends to criticise, not flatter, and the barrier of ice can build up around her quicker than he intended.

VIRGO WOMAN – LIBRA MAN

The Libran man is charmed by mental brightness and sparkling, romantic eyes. His ideals are driven by dreams and beautiful women and, when he meets a gentle, rather sweet and feminine Virgo girl, he will immediately, and quite thoughtlessly, plunge into an affair with love. It's easy for him, and it happens often, but really this time he should have known better. The Virgo woman is usually very careful about who she allows into her space, and the easy-going and rather romantic man who walks through her door will enchant her with his abstract mind, and considerate judgments of the world. The Virgo woman, however, can sense that he prevaricates more than he thinks. He is an extrovert, and demands the security of people around him, which she doesn't. He will begin to grumble when she nit-picks at and criticises his friends, and when she says she would rather he stayed at home more and not play the romantic with every girl he meets. To be so charming is fine when she is on the other end of the flirt, but to see him playing the same tune to other women is, for a Virgo, the shortest route to total frigidity.

The Libran man believes that the Virgo girl is happy with her lot, while he wanders off to socialise. But these girls are not quite as home-loving as they seem, and would rather build a career than actually go and do the shopping. They both enjoy a pleasant, comfortable lifestyle with no heavy scenes, but the Libran doesn't take easily to commitments, any choice implies rejecting the alternative. And if it's a toss up between freedom and the Virgo lady, it will be a decision that he will probably never make. But she will!

VIRGO MAN – SCORPIO WOMAN

The inquiring nature of the Virgo man can seem trifling in comparison with the penetrating, all-power-seeking probing of the Scorpio woman. The Virgo man lives to find a woman who can provide him with mental stimulation and practical support. He is strong, but he needs to feel strength around him so that it is real. The Scorpio woman will immediately love the Virgo man's level-headed and analytical mind. She will be attracted both to his romantic nature and to his practical one. Scorpio women are emotional and determined. Their strength is their character, and the whole of their life is lived with purpose, both for love and for life. The Virgo man may find this hard to live with. He doesn't exactly enjoy emotional scenes of any kind, and he certainly can't cope with the pressures that a Water sign like Scorpio can turn on him in her most passionate moments.

He would like to be enlightened by her tremendous power to inject all kinds of feeling into her love-making but somehow he is never quite there with her. He will be dexterous, agile and know every position under the sun, but he won't be able to provide her with the solution to love, and the universe, which is essentially what this woman wants from her sex life. Virgo believes sex to be pure. It is an art to be perfected, it does not have any deeper meaning to his life. Sadly, this involves not a jot of the emotional content that a Scorpio woman reads into every move he makes. They can quite easily misunderstand one another, even while they enjoy being together but, after a while, she will become too demanding, and the Virgo is more likely to suffer with headaches, turn on the cold shower too often, and resort to a high-powered fault-finding mission to recuperate.

VIRGO WOMAN – SCORPIO MAN

Now the Virgo woman does enjoy submission at times; not often, because she is a very proud and careful practitioner and won't be made a fool of easily. But there's something rather sensational about the soulful way the Scorpio waits to move in. A Virgo is not overtly a 'feeling' person, but this man can send shudders down her spine, and melt her poise before she's even felt the sting of his tail. They may meet and spend a long time being attracted to each other without either of them summoning up the courage to do anything about it. For all his womanising, the Scorpio prefers the waiting, the lingering and the anticipation of the moment. He is drawn to mystery and darkness. And if he can keep the light out on her inner self for a long time, the more charged his sexual energy will be when it is time to release it. He will be suspicious of her intentions at first – he is suspicious of daylight too. Virgo women are pretty good at mental sharpness and, like barbed wire, a Scorpio can become caught up in her mind. Usually he moves in and wipes out his victims with vows and promises of passion and fulfilment. This may tempt her, but her Earthy, practical nature will always keep clarity in her visions. Both have an ability to appear cold and unfeeling. Hers is to avoid emotion and his is because he feels so intensely that it's easier to keep the true depth of his love hidden, even from himself. If the Virgo girl turns sexually cold on him, which she will do if she suspects he is gathering his strength to form an onslaught on another unsuspecting female, then he will end their relationship with sadistic pleasure.

VIRGO MAN – SAGITTARIUS WOMAN

The communication is good between these two rather oddly matched signs. The Sagittarius girl seeks freedom and love. Finding the paradox is her quest in life, and the Virgo man can understand this mentality, because it is a thinking process he can analyse and act upon. To a poised, unruffled Virgo man, the wild and extremist behaviour of Fire signs usually fascinates him to begin with and then, after a while, irritates him. It's always easier to find fault in strength rather than in weakness. The Archer girl is incredibly adaptable, and so is Virgo. She may think him pedantic and rather too steady for her clattering lifestyle. She will insist on having fun, playing jokes on the man she loves, and generally misbehaving.

Full of surprises, the Archer girl likes to outwit even a Virgo intellectually. This is not something he will get a buzz from, and he will have to prepare himself for the mental red-alert she presents. But the Archer girl's independence and spirit needs a firm shoulder to lean on at times. She has insecurities, but her strength is intuitively knowing what goes on in a Virgo man's head. He may not have much of a heart, but she can stretch it out into the world of romance with extraordinary talent.

Virgos aren't exactly balls of fire in bed. He may not even stir her the way she really wants to be stirred, but he will be romantic and willing to be led on sexual adventures that he never knew existed. He wants to understand her egalitarian and clowning behaviour, and she finds his old-fashioned and stuffy mind an easy prey for her outspoken and blunt humour. They could find an easy rapport in time, but it will be based on friendship, rather than any sexual intimacy.

VIRGO WOMAN – SAGITTARIUS MAN

The sensible and sometimes tight-fisted Virgo girl will find that the Archer's extraordinary generosity and rather lax approach to finances make her squirm with disapproval. She will want more than anything to organise him, and hope that his expansive attitude to money is not the same as it is to women. Unfortunately her hopes may be dashed. The Sagittarius needs to open up his life and take everyone into it, and give it all to the world if he can. And in this respect he really does want to be friends with everyone he meets. Other men are suspicious of such honest and open carelessness and women, of course, are usually convinced that they are the true love of his life. They should beware, especially Virgo women. She may well fall instantly in love with the rogue of the zodiac. It's easy. He is so child-like, so lovable and funny. He's a bit clumsy with his heart, and can be rather big-mouthed and coarse, but he is also honest. And a Virgo girl really gets high on honesty. At first he'll be impressed with her intellect, as bouncy and easy as his own. To a Sagittarian man falling in love is often as sudden as the arrow he's just fired, but another arrow can come angling along and split the first, and the Archer is vulnerable to his own need for freedom. Another woman is freedom from the first, and, although he never means to hurt anyone, he can throw relationships around without thinking, as if they were sharp stones on the road to happiness. He is thoughtless rather than harmful, and the Virgo woman can end up the temporary stop-over on his quest for the ideal woman. And a Sagittarius always has one of those!

VIRGO MAN – CAPRICORN WOMAN

This sensible pair is well matched for any partnership, but essentially it will be a partnership in the style of a business arrangement rather than a love-affair. Both the Virgo Man and the Goat girl are after stability and firm foundations on which to build their mutual need for success. The Capricorn girl can often be more ambitious than her Virgo mate, and this could work very well to her advantage. She has no contest over who leads, and there will be sensible meetings between them, ready to face the boardroom and take the consequences of their actions. However, both are stubborn to varying degrees. She because Goats really are rigid and reserved in their opinions and won't budge if they are goaded. A Virgo will mentally attempt to budge as he enjoys mind-games, but he doesn't like to disagree, nor argue. He likes to put things in their place and let them stay there, unless he feels they may be changed. The Goat girl will find him a bit chilly in the bedroom, but her own desire for privacy and her more important need for a dependable and reliable service (she may treat him rather like a bus timetable) outweigh basic sexuality and love. The Goat may tire of the rather purist tactics the Virgo Man attributes to her success.

Neither is interested in emotion and they will find their rapport will be built on belief in commitment and sharing the good and pleasant things in life. As they grow older together, their bond will be usually unbreakable.

VIRGO WOMAN – CAPRICORN MAN

If a Goat has reached the top of his own special mountain, he might be glad of the respect and admiration that the Virgo girl can give him. He never actually gets too excited about anything apart from personal hard-lining. If this includes making a permanent fixture of the Virgo girl, then he may find he has chosen the best course of action. The road to his success is littered with women who can be useful, carry him up the golden stairway, or leave him cold and bitter. He is a cynic, but the Virgo girl is equally able to understand he's had a few rough and tumble relationships before he met her. But she is convinced that he will find her the perfect, trusting and sensible partner. She won't necessarily want to be his prop, more like his companion. Both strong characters will find much stability in this well-balanced and sensible relationship. She needs to communicate in her own strident way, and he rather likes her fine and highly critical mind. It does enhance his mountain top. She will occasionally unnerve him with her hypercritical nit-picking over breakfast, or the importance of getting to the train on time when he was actually planning a very important take-over bid for the next-door neighbour's building plot. She might have to be wary of his habit as he grows older to play the genial youth. The need for order and for control in his relationship might occasionally be undermined by her pig-headed affront at being treated that way. She is a feminine but strong woman, and he is a very powerful man who needs her.

VIRGO MAN – AQUARIUS WOMAN

The Virgo man is essentially a loner, and the Aquarian girl is mostly everybody's friend. She needs people around as if they are part of her very being. However, the Virgo man, who has taken a keen interest in her extraordinary and unpredictable behaviour, at first might be able to understand her humanitarian and extrovert nature. Aquarian girls like analysing and subjecting people to bold and frank inquiry. It's interesting for her to see how they tick, and whether they get upset by her form of character analysis. Funnily enough, the Virgo man can get quite happy on criticism and analysis too, but on a fussier level.

Mentally they have much in common, but their differences can cause friction and tensions which may never get them further than a first encounter.

Being an Air sign makes the Aquarian girl fairly immune to emotion and also fairly uninterested in sex. She insists on maintaining an awful lot of freedom in her relationships, mostly so that her rebellious and lawless attitude is never subjected to restraint. The Virgo will attempt to let her have free rein, but he won't enjoy the company of friends in the kitchen and on the telephone, or hanging round their flat all hours of the night. He has his routine, and he has his order. She has no routine, the less routine the better, and she loves her chaos.

This can make them either become inextricably fascinated with each other, or separate them quickly. Sex is not something either of them find the core of their lives, so if friendship and partnership are handled carefully they may stick it out. Not an exciting romance, but the chance of a lasting partnership.

VIRGO WOMAN – AQUARIUS MAN

The first thing an Aquarius Man must do is respect that the Virgo girl he's become fascinated by is as independent as he is, but not interested in his friends. This may come as a shock to him, because he really dotes on his friends, more than he possibly would a dog. Why can't she just be another friend? Why does she insist on being someone special? Aquarians don't like to think anyone is more special in their life than themselves. Friends, relatives, spouses, business partners share his equality rule. He will give pleasure to the world with the same amount of attention, and will hope that those around him benefit from his ability to change them. The Virgo woman might not enjoy this at all. She can adapt to anything with great ease, but she won't want to be changed for the sake of change. He will stubbornly exert his contrary opinions upon her most of the time, and she will attempt to remind herself that she saw in him a dreamer, a visionary who could make the world a better place. But he does keep trying so hard to be difficult, and different, and turning a relationship upside down for the sake of it is the kind of tactic to alienate even a Virgo girl.

She is difficult to please too, so there will be times when he will slump off with his friends and ignore any conflict. He can get angry with her nit-picking and the way she has to clean up his chaos. He likes a rather obscure orderliness, one that he has designed. He will choose the most austere furniture, or the most way-out central heating system, refuse to have animals around because he gets allergic to dust and hairs, and stubbornly believes she would be a better woman for his cranky habits. If she can resist criticising his friends and accept that she will never be the only woman in his unorthodox life, then he might just agree to try eating toast in the morning instead of a piece of lettuce.

VIRGO MAN - PISCES WOMAN

The Fish girl is by nature sensitive, sweet and gentle, but she also has a certain Watery deviousness which often pops to the surface like the bubbles from her Fishy gills. The times that these slippery and spicier facets of this woman arise is usually when she's met a Virgo man. Virgo men have this uncanny ability either to bring out the worst in a girl (usually if she's one the Water signs) or the best (another Earth). Of course what happens to the Air and Fire signs is up to them! The Piscean girl meeting the rather mean and uncompromising Virgo with a wad of cash and no one to spend it on, can become masochistically infatuated with his very tight personality. The Virgo hangs out his role of perfect lover as a Daz advert exposes the whiteness that it claims is unique to Daz. But the Fish can see right through this charade. Beneath that perfect-gentleman act is a man who is an idealist and one who is in love with purity. He will immediately believe she is the purest form of woman. Not only is she a dreamer, wistful and difficult to catch, she is not interested in his robotic seduction. He hasn't, of course, the intuition or sixth sense that she has to realise she is being the rather slippery character that often mermaids are.

When he finally beavers in to claim her, to seduce her with words which have a finer chance of working than just male lust, he might just find that their sexual encounter will bring the true purity that he needs, and the idealistic love that she always feels is waiting. He may find her gregarious nature clashes with his rather lonely one, but she feels deeply, and will usually come back to listen to him with an open heart.

VIRGO WOMAN – PISCES MAN

For a while, when he comes dripping out of the ocean in search of romance on solid ground, the Fish will realise that there are very few true and pure women, very few ideals are ever better than the ones you can dream. But as he slithers on to the shoreline of the Virgo girl's quite sharp and bright-eyed affection, he will begin to wonder if maybe dreams can be made on dry land.

He will be wary of her rather private, solitary way of life. His own is friendly and humane and, although he is renowned for his disappearances into lonely woods and solitary seashores, he actually needs people very much. There will be arguments between Virgo and her Fish because the Piscean is basically a ditherer, always vague and not quite ready to make a definite commitment, either verbally, or emotionally. Virgo on the other hand wants to know the truth and will pull him to pieces with her caustic mouth, if he messes around too long.

But she faces another nagging problem. She really hates spending money, and he loves spending it. When she realises that his extravagance can lead him to be addictive in many of the more escapist pleasures of life, she will try desperately to stop him. But the Fish can turn cold and unresponsive if anyone throws too many demands on his sensitive scales.

She can be the seductress in his bed, and the restrictive force in his life. He will enjoy her romantic side but will have to tolerate the restraints she imposes on his natural freedom. And Fish are better at tolerating than Virgos. She will need his gentle sexuality. His dreamy, always mystical and faraway love-making. They may be mutually fulfilled if they learn to see in one another what is lacking within themselves.

VIRGO MAN – ARIES WOMAN

The outgoing and tactless Ram girl can seem quite a viable proposition for the Virgo idealist looking for perfection. To be able to control this headstrong woman would seem to him a rather invigorating and mentally challenging business, as long as she doesn't attempt to wash his socks, because he always does it *his* way, and makes sure she cleans up every crumb from the bed before he gets into it.

The Virgo man is sometimes unsure of what his ideal is. When he meets an Aries he is, of course, initially infatuated with her very opposite fantasy to his own. But her mystery, however enticing it is to him, can crumble into truth and become an irritant rather like those breadcrumbs between the sheets.

An Aries woman will find his cold, unyielding purity not at first an attraction. But he could be the sort of man she might recklessly have a frantic love-affair with, or just forget him all together. Yet there is something rather strangely magnetic between these two, and often an Aries girl will push back the frontiers of the Antarctic and storm into his heart to try to find if the ice is meltable on her own very high temperature gauge. The Virgo may find her irresistible, while the romantic perfectionist is working overtime. His performance in bed will win her over for a while but once the initial sexual encounter has diminished between them, there is very little left for them to salvage except her independence and his digestive problems.

VIRGO WOMAN – ARIES MAN

Now we all know that Virgos have a thing about perfection. Not the heady, sensitive perfection of a Piscean dreamer, but a practical, down-to-earth belief that there is someone out there who can provide a Virgo with her heart's desire. Now an Aries out for an entanglement, sexual or otherwise, turning on his favourite virility lesson, can seem the kind of hedonistic turn-on that a Virgo will find both alluring and repellent. The Aries Ram will pick her up for her femininity, think he can save her from a life of dull routine, and is sure she must find him the most beautiful creature. (Fire signs have a rather naïve vanity.) He won't be fond of her cold and rational resentment, although he's got his own jealousy to contend with too. The Aries man will be amused by the Virgo woman's sharp, subtle mentality, and he'll get infatuated with the apparent Earthiness of her sexuality. But don't believe that it will keep him coming back for more unless she can inspire him with a bit more heady passion than financial considerations or whether she defrosted the fridge and left the door open. The Virgo girl will want to organise him from day one, and this man really doesn't like anything to be organised, let alone himself!

The coldness of her passion won't be their only obstacle to success. She has this awful ability to appear to disapprove of all the Aries man's most genuine and child-like qualities. He is chaotic, fun-loving, impetuous and risky. She is ordered, a worrier, sensible and concerned with purity, not passion. She is a lover of romance but, once the romance has gone, she is happy to work hard for a good solid relationship based on how she sees a perfect marriage. Never mind what the Aries man thinks, as far as she is concerned he doesn't think, he merely acts. And the Ram's actions don't usually speak loud enough for her analytical and precise mind.

VIRGO MAN – TAURUS WOMAN

The Virgo man is hypercritical of most women, but there's something very pleasant and comforting about the Taurean girl. It's as if she's as perfect as a woman could possibly be, and that's a standard he rarely believes he'll find. These two usually meet at work, rather than at play. The Virgo man does little playing and that which he does won't usually involve places where he can be tempted by women.

His hunt for perfection will often lead him to question the Bull's placid nature and strength of purpose and, when he realises that he can't pick many holes in her character, he will decide, meticulously, and analytically that therefore she must be the most suitable candidate available. He is known to fall in love, but it's a quiet, emotionless experience. Romance is easy for him, because it involves no thread of emotion, only lines from a book. The Taurus girl will think this man a prig at first, conceited, over-obsessive and the plaintive for cold and unresponsive pedantry. Yet when she realises he's got the same motivation and determination, that in fact he is quite resilient and is happy to clarify every situation with analysis, she might even uncover a subtle depth to the sensible way he folds his pyjamas. (A lot of Virgo men do still wear pyjamas, and like them to be ironed.) A domestic-minded Taurus will get on better with him than a career girl but, if she can show enterprise and initiative, not cause emotional scenes, stamp her feet, or leave too many pairs of tights round the bathroom, he might just feel content with her.

Sexually he can seem cold, and she might take a while to warm him up. But if anyone can, a Taurean's basic sensuality will get him off on a different planet than he's ever known. Could she be the perfection he's been looking for?

VIRGO WOMAN – TAURUS MAN

So you've heard that two Earth signs together makes one big heap of volatile compost? Well, in some respects you're right.

Taurus and Virgo have the same approach to life. Unfortunately the difference is that the Virgo girl has a discriminating approach to sex and love, and Taurus doesn't. The Bull is down-to-earth, but probably too hedonistic for the Virgo girl when it comes to all the Earthy pleasures he needs to indulge in. Virgo girls like to analyse sex. Perfection between the sheets is what they want, not the snore of a Bull at dawn and smelly socks on the pillow. The basic raw attitude to life of a Bull is actually not very satisfactory to a Virgo, unless she can control him, and organise him without his even noticing that she is! Taurus isn't a fusspot and doesn't care if the duvet cover wasn't washed since Sunday as long as the bed is comfortable and he gets enough sleep. He can be intolerably untidy, and a Virgo is incredibly tidy-minded. She may actually like the Bull's mess, and choose to clear it up or ignore it, as long as it is ordered chaos, then it's OK. He could actually provide the Virgo girl with her delight for cleaning up and worrying about his dirty collars, and she could be the answer to his sloppy living.

Virgo girls need romance, pretty linen sheets, flowers on

their birthday and champagne, which sometimes the Bull forgets, and finds her desires hard to cope with. If their relationship isn't a purely physical one, then it would be better for them both. In fact these two Earth signs make an excellent marriage and then, at least, the Virgo will have something more to criticise than just the Bull's slobbing in bed till noon.

VIRGO MAN – GEMINI WOMAN

The precision-timer of the zodiac will get quickly frustrated when he meets a Gemini woman, mainly because her time-keeping is her own law. If she says she will meet him at eight she will usually bump into an old friend and chat for an hour before she remembers to call him. Her ability to go off at tangents and attempt the impossible and be in two places at once is part of her Mercurial charm.

The Virgo man has little Mercurial charm, he has all the practicalities it imposes on life. Of course, he is a perfectionist, requires a normal amount of affection and a large amount of logic in his love-affairs, but really can't waste his precious time with a girl who changes her personality and her job more frequently than a kaleidoscope changes colour.

Virgo men are quite adept at the first inklings of romance. They like to believe they are better at picking up a girl than any other sign. However, because they secretly yearn for a wife, rather than a lover, the Gemini girl will not be awfully good at this kind of partnership. They have little in common, and sexually they will probably flounder fairly soon after any initial infatuation has subsided. The Twins hate to be cornered, and the Virgo man is essentially quite keen on cornering and then dissecting the female of his attention. She may fall for this the first few times, but eventually even the lightness of a Virgo sexual encounter can bore her.

VIRGO WOMAN – GEMINI MAN

Not a relationship on which dreams are made. The Gemini man certainly won't want to enrich his life with hyper-criticism and meticulous analysis of why he didn't arrive dead on nine o'clock when he was supposed to. The Virgo girl will find herself constantly suspicious, and probably on red-alert if he so much as decides to travel anywhere without her. She will also find it hard to understand why he is so casual and so laid-back about life. At first when they meet romantically it might be all birds and bees. They share the same mutability, the same restless desire for knowledge, except the Gemini will actively seek change and love change and the Virgo would rather sit down and dwell on it, and then organise it within the compartments she's chosen. Her orderly mind gets the Gemini man reaching for his suitcase pretty quickly. He hates to be told what to do and the Virgo girl loves telling people what to do. He also won't want to take the future or their relationship too seriously. Romance is all very well, it has an ending in sight, but a future with a paradigm of virtue sounds to him like the sweetest icing on the biggest wedding-cake. And you know how he hates weddings!

Sexually they have little in common. He is cool, and can fluctuate between sex in his head and no sex. She is in need of romance, of affection, and an Earthy lightness, rather than a mental one. Their Mercury ruler may give them the same ability to analyse and dissect, but the Virgo will turn it to fault-finding and the Gemini will turn it to wondering what he is doing in bed with this serious woman in the first place.

VIRGO MAN – CANCER WOMAN

The Virgo man seeks perfection in a woman. Occasionally he comes across a woman who, he thinks, may be answer to this niggling problem, but very rarely. The Crab lady certainly appears the sweetest, most charming, feminine and deeply emotional woman he has ever met, but there is something he can't quite reason about her. And he does love to reason everything. The Crab girl has the same approach to life and money as the Virgo in many ways. They both like to look after their money, and they both need to maintain a certain privacy in their personal lives. The Virgo man, however, is cold emotionally and, although the Moon girl has her frigid moments, she needs a warmth that might not be returned from this rather old-fashioned and hyper-critical man. He worries too much about his health, and the Moon woman will know every cure in the book, intuitively she will be able to sense his headache coming on, will reach for the aspirins before he's even noticed and be at his side with a port and brandy when he's got a sneeze. They both are very attentive towards each other, but the Virgo's perfection-seeking might begin to niggle her. The Crab won't be able to take his caustic comments for long, and she certainly won't like to be organised like a telephone directory. There will be many breakdowns in their sexual communication. For although the Crab is perceptive, the Virgo can get mighty restless about being in the same bed as anyone, even the one who he thought was so perfect. He does like his crisp white sheets, and the window open in the winter. The Crab will quickly retreat and the Virgo will cool down, and the sexual perfectionist might even turn to celibacy if he feels that the Moon girl has abandoned his ice-box.

VIRGO WOMAN – CANCER MAN

Modesty and refinement walk hand-in-hand usually. One will support the other and they both will work hard to carry and share the load. With a Crab man and a Virgo girl there is a lot of modesty on both sides, and mostly refinement from the Virgo tastes in life. They may first meet through a third party. Cancer men don't often pick up girls, and Virgo women are very fussy about who they talk to. A Crab will, as usual, be extremely cautious about revealing the darker side of his nature. He will flirt his extrovert side around quite casually and the Virgo girl can be genuinely infatuated by the bright, strong leadership quality of this sensitive and genuine man. She likes genuine people, honesty and truth. The Virgo girl will then settle down to analyse the Cancerian man. After much deliberation, she reaches a decision that he may actually suffer from emotional trauma, he is affected by the Moon, but she can understand why his behaviour can change with his moods. She will suggest a relationship that can be assured permanence. He will admire her for her mental and highly intellectual reasoning power. It seems she's the sort of girl he needs, a woman who can remind him of the logic behind his deep and complicated search for truth, and someone who can keep him secure and contented. He may find after a while that her analysing turns to criticism, and that her bright and fresh intellect is too crisp and clear-cut for his more emotional swaying one. Sexually they will complement each other unless her Virgo criticism extends to the bedroom and then the Cancer will turn as frigid and cold as the Moon.

VIRGO MAN – LEO WOMAN

Practicalities are the same as perfection to the Virgo man. He needs order and neatness, he needs to feel in control, and he needs a conservative and simple lifestyle. He may hang his pyjamas over the chair every night and brush his teeth for exactly two minutes. He may keep a digital clock and a mechanical one, just in case one is fast. If he gets into a conversation with a Leo lady, he may surprise himself that he finds her gushing and flamboyant chatter quite entertaining. He is rather serious in life and here is a ravishing, fun-loving girl who is ready to flirt everyone under the table. Their attraction will emanate from curiosity. His because she is so ridiculous, and hers because he is so staid and neat. The likelihood that she will fall in love with him is slim, it could happen because he was playing the perfect-lover role, which is his only role and a good one at that. And also because his head is full of the most incredible things, not the sort of things a Leo will necessarily need in her own ostentatious brain, but different, concise, like a concise dictionary rather than the compendium of life with which the Leo lady believes she is blessed. She thinks she knows everything, but she needs warmth too. The Virgo man is cold and *really* knows everything. That is what they have in common. He is sensitive, for all his apparent coldness. Unless she gets her pride hurt, she may never be aware of this side of his nature. Her attempt at playing the leading-lady in his life might set him with an interesting mental spiral but it will quickly make him dizzy. She won't want to be the wife with the grace he expected, nor will she want to time his egg, nor be punctual for their dinner parties.

Sexually she'll surprise him often. She has passion, is full of passion, and he will still be looking up the next position in the *Kama Sutra* if she hasn't left him first. He is dexterous and believes he has mastered the art of sex like a true technician. But Leo ladies don't want technicians in their beds, they want a star act.

VIRGO WOMAN – LEO MAN

Virgos are for ever trying to improve on what they have, to perfect their own high standards. If they get involved with a Lion along the way, then that might just as well involve improving the Lion to their own meticulous flow-chart. The problem for the delicate pedantry of the Virgo romantic is that Leos don't usually fit into any improvement programme. For a start they are already better than anyone in bed, around the house, intellectually, and with money. In relationships they convince themselves that they know how to make it work, and a Leo man will certainly not listen to a woman who thinks she knows best. He would rather show the Virgo how to enjoy life, living for each moment, rather than running around worrying about it. She might go along with this idea, for a while, but she won't tolerate his terrible untidiness and his constant need to work either like it's the last day he has on earth, or play every game until he's won. His loyalty will impress her, but her attempts to clean the ring round the bath every time he has one, will hurt his pride. He doesn't like to be reminded he's left his books all over the house, and really can't see what it's got to do with her anyway. The chances of them getting this far in their relationship are slim. The Virgo will, at the outset, play her feminine charm, her quiet side, quite naturally. But she will want to criticise, and she will want to instil her ideals on this rather bold presumptuous and prattling man. He's just the type to listen isn't he? Unfortunately, Leos only listen to themselves, and can get hard-of-hearing quite easily if they feel their dignity is threatened. She will inspire him to tenderness in bed though, albeit not quite the passion he needs to ignite his full attention. Mentally she'll be challenging, but once she begins to clock him into the house and out of it, he may well begin to wonder what happened to his Cat-flap.

Virgo

PREDICTIONS
October 1994 – December 1995

♍

OCTOBER 1994

The aspirations to perfection that any Virgo must have felt were beginning to wear thin should, at last, this month resolve themselves with the knowledge that, however difficult it is to form close and personal relationships, there comes a time when you are ready to break through caution and accept people for what they are and not what you would like them to be. October sees the chance for you to communicate any worries and fears to someone special, without the need to observe closely each reaction or action of their body language, or mental gestures towards you. For once you may begin to discriminate with a genuine love, rather than a diffident analysis. Measuring every reaction against your idea of perfection can often seem time-wasting and trivial to many of your distant acquaintances and friends. The new Moon on the 5th reminds you that your own interests, and your own possessions, however uncluttered and thin on the ground, must be looked after first, before you start to analyse the needs of others. Putting your own house in order is one of the key contentments to stabilising your obsessional mind. By the 7th, with a charming aspect between the Moon and Venus, you may at least be able to talk amongst friends or close partners and articulate your thoughts again. Reviewing other people's lives is frankly one of your more critical and meticulous ways of testing whether they live up to your standards of perfection. In most relationships you often verge near the truth when you discriminate between those who are worthy of your friendship and those who are not. Allowing others to express their beliefs and their convictions without your criticism can only put you closer to them. Cold and distant friendships are safer, but they dilute the truth. Your ruler, Mercury, although winging its way currently through the area of your chart relating to your feelings as well as your possessions, might enable you to take the opportunity to pass one of your own highly qualified examinations in the art of good relationships!

♍

NOVEMBER 1994

The silence of love in your heart is only ever fanned and drawn out when you feel secure and able to distance yourself from emotion in your mind. As long as your mental assimilation of the facts is valid then, if your heart stumbles, at least you are able to recover the pieces and place them precisely back into the boxes from which they fell. The struggle you have been going through to communicate your deep and rather reclusive heart is now being broached heavily by others with more emotion and greater heat in their spirits. But this month, with a fair and beneficial series of aspects in the area of your chart relating to airing thoughts and feelings, you should be in a better position than ever to express what you really mean, however muted and cold it may seem to a close partner or friend. Modest in outlook, you are also modest in words and deeds, and it might solve the agony of someone else's confusion if, this month, you bend the rules slightly and let modesty slide by the wayside. It seems the time has come to give more and express more than usual. Once your ruler Mercury glides into Scorpio on the 10th, you will breathe a sigh of relief, and your worries and fears will be made easy by the return of your smooth and cool approach to a close partner's frustration. A considerate aspect between Venus and Mercury will also ensure that you are firmly in control. Although Mercury rules Virgo, as it does Gemini, it is with the embers of Mercury's hot feet that you analyse and dissect truths. Mercury himself has left your heel-prints on fire, and has already dashed ahead to face new challenges that are for the Gemini spirit. Your mode of communication is to provide the critique of experiences rather than be the outrider or the doer. Like the art critic in the daily newspaper, you believe you are set with the task of analysing the good and the bad in everyone. Everyone, that is, apart from you! November may be full of arguments and, perhaps, a number of serious mental conflicts around the 19th and 20th, when the Sun makes two powerful aspects to Jupiter and Pluto, but the former only serve to emphasise that, by opening up and generating expression, rather than finding economy in it, you may put the truth on the line for once. With the Sun conjuncting Pluto, you may find that the self-expression has turned method to madness and you could be in need of purging your own mind rather than others'!

♍

DECEMBER 1994

The urge to find the purest form of experience, and the driving force of Virgo's self-serving instinct often makes you seem cool as ice, and many find it hard to spring the trip-wire of warmth in your heart. But this month, now that you have let off steam, in the most economical way of course, you may feel that the home front would benefit from the same analysis and inspection as your own rather emotionally cold motives. With Jupiter moving into its own sign on the 9th, you might begin to clarify and widen your horizons, and take your very personal and private home life out into the world. Although not a truly social animal, you do enjoy a few friends around you, even though you keep them at a cold distance. You hate large, noisy parties and prefer intellectual companions rather than boisterous ones. But you often go to other extremes and enjoy theatres or large, anonymous gatherings where you can scrutinise your companions with the sort of telescopic opera-glasses that reveal their many and fascinating habits!

A lightness glares at the end of the rather introverted tunnel this month and, as Christmas approaches, on the 19th Mercury enters the area of your chart related to lighter romance, flirtations and the finer pleasures of life. Although never passionate about life, you are a romantic, in the purist and idealist sense of the word and, with the Sun also entering Capricorn on the 22nd, you may begin to feel that there is more than routine and responsibility in your life and it is time to make light of any festivity and fun, even in your rather pragmatic way. Even pragmatists can turn their routine into delicate and tidy love, and you'd be surprised when, after the Moon has thrown a moody restraint on any close relationship on the 9th, how you suddenly receive an energising boost to your ego by the Moon and Mars in the area of your chart relating to the self. It is time for you to realise that magic and romance can also seem the purest form of experience, as long as you keep a watchful eye on every reaction you have!

♍
JANUARY 1995

Still scorching in the embers of Mercury's hot-heeled rush into Aquarius, you may, for the first few weeks of the year, feel comfortable in your recent brush with romance. The apparent routine and commitments you enjoy so much are channelling your energy wisely. However, the Sun is still high in Capricorn and your attempts to economise on feeling may clash with your New Year's resolution to suppress any emotional challenge for the future. To have become, even for a while, extravagant with your moods may also encourage you to bring on a new complaint that whoever is responsible for your current and rather unusual conflict of mind and heart, should be blamed. Believing that someone is at fault is part of the process of your exaggerated need for perfection. This month you could find fault both with friends, when, on the 16th, you may engage in an unusual and rather sudden social encounter with a wider number of people than usual, and also with yourself, when, on the 21st, the Sun finally enters the area of your chart related to routines and workloads and you may be convinced that your restless brain is not up to its meticulous high standards!

Your energy level should be at its highest at the beginning of January but, once Mars turns retrograde into Leo on the 23rd, you might feel even more withdrawn and decide to neutralise any ideals of anarchy in your head and turn back to the still spirit within.

♍

FEBRUARY 1995

Your obsession with a tidy house, and often a tidy mind, can spill over at times into your relationships. If a partner or friend is as ordered as you, and lives up to your highly critical analysis, then you may expect the same standards from others which you yourself can often not possibly attain. You often draw a psychological barrier between yourself and reality and, because you would rather live in the cold than the heat, you can seem sober and quite often abnormally conventional. Yet you yearn for the sweetness and chasteness of first love and romance, and it looks very likely that this month could see the start of such a light and pure relationship, particularly if you are single. Any Virgos already in partnerships may find that they become more aware of the delicacy of the romance that was the first inspiration to love, before their relationship changed to routine and daily neatness. Venus enters the area of your chart related to romance and creative and pleasure pursuits, with the lightness and froth of sentiment. With your usual adherence to time-keeping and your need for intellectual rapport, you may initially enjoy only a light flirtation in your head, rather than with any sexual intention. However, in any encounter into the realm of love, you are immediately suspicious and may either form an immediate and often highly restrictive opinion, or you may analyse your own feelings and attempt to sublimate them. As you carry little of the past with you, it is easy for you to adapt and take in new situations. As each event occurs you appraise and exert your own judgment as to its value in your environment. Sometimes, because of this you see only what you want to see, and this month you may well find your insensitivity carries you through the romance and sentiment into an area that you usually treat with much trepidation. Now as the Sun enters Pisces on the 19th and, on the 26th, Venus conjuncts Neptune, feelings of an intensely idealistic and intuitive romantic nature may be enjoyed and measured against your own personal reactions. Partnerships now have the greatest chance of working, or, at least, already established ones can be reassessed for their pure love.

♍

MARCH 1995

Losing sight of the overall landscape can often bring into view wrong perspectives and wrong critical analyses of the situation. Losing sight of the forest for the extraordinary twig on the tree that must be meticulously researched for

every living organism, is often how you spark love into
action and how you respond to it. When it goes wrong,
you blame without consideration, and often wrongly. The
restless yearnings of the past few weeks may now be firmly
matched to one examination of yourself you had never
anticipated. The new Moon on the 1st falls in the area of
your chart where you are sensitive to love, and towards a
close partner or relationship. With a powerful aspect
between the Sun and Saturn on the 5th, you may feel the
economy of your own need to restrain emotion and to
perfect your resolve, along with the desire that has been
building in your heart over a new-found relationship.
Moods and emotions are not often fondly welcomed into
your heart, and this month you may experience the strain
of worrying about feeling at all! It is part of your nature to
worry about most things, and restless activity often results.
You may find an emotional cord that is being tightened
round your neck is not under your scrutiny, nor under the
microscope where you wanted it to be. Yet even you are
open to infatuation and persuasion, especially when
Mercury makes a splendid aspect to the Moon on the 29th
and you at last begin to let go of your hyper-critical stance
and let a little more unconventional behaviour into your
life. Friends may see you loosened and freer from your own
self-critical efficiency than you have been for a long time.
After the Moon and Venus conjunction of the 28th, you
may come to some realisation that your notions of love are
similar to, and may be compatible with, those of a romantic
partner – an attachment you never believed would be
possible.

♍

APRIL 1995

To analyse the romance and infatuation of any relationship
is often what leads to its downfall. But as you are an
amiable pedant and perfectionist, you are always first to

dissect and grind every reaction and response to the finest grain that can be put under the microscope of your inquiring mind. Yet by doing so you often miss the true and spiritual significance of any relationship. Preferring a colder relationship is often your means of avoiding the hearts that live within and, although you are enlivened and invigorated by close sexual encounters, and the physical attraction that always precedes any solid relationship, there is still a part of you that remains well hidden from reality. Because you prefer it to stay there!

The beginning of the month suggests that much should be done to enhance a new relationship, or to improve an old one, with regard to the sexuality and energy that you can create. With Mercury entering the area of your chart relating to the very private and special life-force and sexual energy that can be awakened by love, you may find that at last you are able to open your feeling to reason and offer more than intellectual and routine companionship. A wonderful conjunction between Mercury and the Sun around the 14th, in the sexual area of your chart, emphasises not only that you should communicate your physical desires, but that you should also act upon them rather than analysing every move you make! Because you lack drive and can sometimes take a long time to make decisions, it is often up to your partner to provide the propeller for getting any physical or emotional contact going. In many light and brief affairs you have, of course, perfected the art of love-making and of playing the Romeo or Juliet! But because, inevitably, you are more interested in intellectual stimulation and companionship, the rest of love's offerings often come later rather than sooner. But with so much current planetary activity in those areas of your chart where love and sex are motivated, or changed for the better, you may at last feel that the weight of commitment and the playing of love-games is finally removed from your shoulders. It may seem like the simple and clock-watching lifestyle you prefer to live can at last be genuinely shared with someone who actually accepts you on your own terms.

♍

MAY 1995

A mixed month, whereby the first weeks see sexuality playing a testing role in your life and, by the last week, career ambitions and expanding your interests and routines more widely bring you, for a moment, face-to-face with any emotional problems, and then draw you away from them with great and consummate ease. Preferring to avoid emotional and sexual matters often makes any problems relating to them worse, especially for your partner. Even though you have felt the lightness of romance and security, you may not have the time this month even to have a moment to analyse any insecurities. Although your ambitions are slow to develop, with your love of work and routine, they are always carefully crafted and put to a punctual and rigorous timescale. One such moment has occurred this month, when keeping to schedule and a deadline becomes increasingly important and takes up most of your reasoning hours. You may feel the pressure of any close and personal relationship has temporarily shifted out of your microscopic vision and, feeling more at ease, and less self-conscious in the world, you can verify your own desires. Being very aware of self, you prefer the background scenery where you can work to your best advantage rather than any limelight. This spills over into your personal life and, although you want to be the guiding force and guiding light in other people's lives, you never let it appear so. Always to know best is one of your infallible and insistent characteristics and, this month, you may have to show partners and loved ones that, just because you have no time for their personal demands, it is only because you are planning and working both for their and your future that you have economised on love. The Full Moon on the 14th gives you the opportunity to express these thoughts and instigate these feelings, but it won't be until Mars enters your own sign on the 26th that any worries you have incurred this month begin to disperse. Mars brings a new energising force, and you may feel spirited and ready to deal with emotional and domestic problems, although you would rather make sure they were compartmentalised before you had to cope with them!

♍

JUNE 1995

It is more often the case that you would rather travel through life with little sentimental or emotional baggage and tread an eternal path through a land of tasks to be accomplished rather than dreams to be fulfilled. Perhaps this month, with a surprising and challenging aspect between Jupiter and the Sun on the 1st, you may find that home life and your ambitions don't particularly see eye-to-eye. The difficult aspect between Mars and the Moon on the 5th may have put a dampener on your initial energy, when close partners will insist that their emotions and feelings should come first in your relationship.

Although you are normally able to discriminate with great clarity between what others want out of life, and what you think is best for them to have, this month you may find that your usual restless energy is put to the test, and you have to pull all your mental resources out of the bag and take stock of what close partners really want from you. Your ability to communicate on any practical and elemental level is unsurpassed but, when it comes to deeper feelings, you are often reserved and delicate in any confrontation.

The Full Moon on the 13th in Sagittarius signifies a

clarity of vision about the problems you may encounter in the home. With Mercury in a pleasant aspect to Venus on the 19th, you should at least be able to reach an intellectual conclusion about your ambitions and motives at work and at home, although you may not reach any emotional ones yet with your partner or close relationship!

♍
JULY 1995

The satisfying aims of your life may take a new course this month when you begin to feel that friends and acquaintances have returned to your camp. Not known for your outgoing nature, you rely only on a few and mistrust many. How your leisure time is spent in those few precious moments when you temporarily close down your mind for relief are rigorously worked out. Jogging round the block every morning to clock in at the right second is not apparently fun to anyone else but a precise and meticulous attempt to keep yourself fit and then worry about it!

 This month, with Venus in Cancer on the 5th and Mercury speeding its way through Cancer from the 11th, you may enjoy more amusements if you make the time, and this could possibly be the result of the stress and strain of last month's conscience-searching and nit-picking discussions. Partners may insist you get out and have more fun and, although you prefer not to mingle with intimate friends for long, you may enjoy a varied social calendar and lose yourself in the distance of free-range acquaintances. The 12th seems likely to be a day which may set the mood for the rest of the month, when the Full Moon in Capricorn makes a sensitive and delicate aspect to Neptune that illuminates your need for romance and perhaps brings pleasures of love and infatuation hurtling back to your reality. It is hardly surprising, therefore, as the month ends that, although you have enjoyed the company of your friends, you are relieved to get back on terms with your own feelings, and put them in their place, however inspiring romance can be!

♍
AUGUST 1995

Preferring method to madness, this month you may find that at last you are in control of your plans and affairs, rather than letting others take the guiding hand. Although you would prefer to know precisely where you are heading, you are able to handle matters and adapt when the going gets tough. Your ability to put bad times behind you and to forget the past is incomparable. You are neither power-mad nor egotistic, but you have moments when your ego must be allowed to score in the form of mental and intellectual conceit. For most of this month you could find that your ability to win in any intellectual capacity will override the needs of close partners, and much of your modest and, at times, self-effacing thinking could change and take a rather harder and colder critical approach.

The Full Moon on the 10th may make your usual spirit for routine tasks below par, and you would be wise to avoid conflict with any loved one on this occasion. But, with the Sun, Venus, and Mercury all in your own sign for most of this month, there is no one who is able to change your pursuit for the truth, and the cause for the purist and perfectionist path you are now set to follow. If finding perfection in a relationship is an exaggerated aim, then it will manifest itself most powerfully this month, and no one else can turn you against yourself. Even a close partner may find it hard to challenge your delicate enterprise when, on the 22nd, Mercury makes a hard aspect with Saturn and whatever restrictions have been imposed on your relationships, you should now at least feel the intellectual truth behind them.

♍
SEPTEMBER 1995

Fussing and worrying about every niggle in your daily life could draw to a firm and conclusive halt this month, before the fresh and maybe alarming air of the autumn sets a new pace and rigour to your emotional and personal relationships. But this month brings with it peace and contentment in yourself: a time when you can relax and sit back and reflect upon that low profile you prefer. Any economy of expression is a good one, and now not to indulge in intellectual games can only restore and revitalise your brain cells, ready for the Lilliputian onslaught that is about to have a more marked effect on you. The tidy, purist kind of love that you live for has temporarily been grounded and, with it, your heart has been left in the lost-luggage department. The Sun is still in your own sign until the 23rd and this can only enhance and treat your ego to a spark more self-reliance and less self-consciousness. Keeping a wary eye on yourself and your motives is done as wisely as any owl keeps a sharp eye on the ground for mice. Yet this month you may be a little less observant, like an owl with only one eye. The Full Moon in Pisces intensifies a partner's feelings for you, and they may begin to feel the need to make or break the testing strength of your relationship. Blaming someone is better, as far as you are concerned, than holding no one responsible. Your greatest stumbling-block is blame. And this month, as you begin to recover your mental synthesis, and attempt to analyse your partner's grievances, you may feel uncomfortably aware that maybe it is both of you who are to blame. On the 24th the new Moon in Libra puts you into a mood of introspection, and you are ready to pull your own feelings out of the lost-property office to try to discern which are the true ones and which are just floaters!

A gentle aspect between Venus and the Moon on the 25th sheds a new light on your feelings too and, by the end of the month, you are at last able to see more clearly beyond the microscopic data you have gathered. Just this once you could really find out whether it is love you feel, or just satisfaction!

♍ OCTOBER 1995

This month you may struggle against criticism from others. However much you dissect and find fault in your partner's or loved ones' motives and lifestyle, it is with great personal antagonism that you react to criticism turned upon yourself. Convinced most of the time that you are above reproach, there seems little doubt that, if friends or partners resolve to fault-finding, then they are surely not worthy of your precise and perfect nature. Both the Sun and Venus are currently playing games in Scorpio with your mental and communicative methods, and also the struggle in your conscience about love. As much as you require the ultimate and purest form of experience, it still seems that most relationships have their flaws, however hard you restlessly search for the answer. However, this month you could find that a heady and enticing sexual encounter on the 8th, with the Full Moon glowing and drawing its mood across any physical infatuation, will bring you closer to a moment or more of the ultimate romance. Your belief in purity may be restored, and you might do well to turn your wonderfully analytical mind inward for a while to see how bizarre and meticulous your method to finding an ideal really is. The new Moon on the 24th indicates an ability at least to communicate this to someone special and, with a lovely aspect between the Moon and Jupiter on the 27th, you may at last find an open and expressive contentment at home and your energies can be directed towards positive and lucrative emotion within your daily and home environment.

♍

NOVEMBER 1995

This month sees the actions and reactions that you judged so critically last month finally put into a light of examination and cross-questioning. When friends and close partners begin to get frustrated by your cold approach, you might feel more locked out from their trust than ever before. Yet you only have yourself to blame this time and, even though you will insist on holding yourself responsible, with all the good will in the world, you really do care! A crisp Full Moon on the 7th allows you to investigate and penetrate the wider implications of life and love. And the strong conjunction between Venus and Mars on the 23rd makes you realise that friends and partners may argue their case, but it is you who always dig out the answers and know that you are right. You can now rest your case, and remember to have a lot more fun, if you begin to accept that there is a promise of something more dependable and stable in the wings. With Venus in Capricorn on the 28th, you are about to embark on a series of new romances and pleasures, something that, although you carp on about, and often criticise, you know is always really missing in your life. For once it is time not to hold back on friendship or love, and any firm relationships or romantic associations you have made in the past few months are about to become something bigger and better. Pleasure can be constructive and it can be a release of all that nervous energy stored in your head. Letting go and getting on with the fun in life could make this the most beneficial and exciting phase of the year. As December approaches, you should take the chance to see if you can forget the twigs on the tree just for a while and go for the whole of the forest!

♍

DECEMBER 1995

December glows like the embers of Mercury, and it is within this fading spark that you often find most that rewards you. Although the Full Moon on the 7th puts you into a cautious mode where your future and ambitions lie, you may find that now includes your heart. But a sparkling Mars now enters the part of your chart that relates to fun, pleasure and romantic relationships, and any energy or dynamism will be felt from others, rather than from within, and you can respond to their gaiety with an easier mind. There is nothing you can do to stop someone becoming infatuated with you, and now is the time to remember that you want love as much as anyone else. For a while letting love flow rather than damming it at its source, could be the motivation you need to ensure a happy atmosphere. Mercury, your hot-footed friend, enters Capricorn on the 12th, and socially you might find the festive season has come upon you more quickly than you would have liked. However, with that unusually heady, light and delicate air of romance carrying you through the month as if you hadn't a care in the world you should start to enjoy the fun that you so usually try to avoid. Venus conjuncts Neptune on the 17th and any sensitive and idealistic feelings you may have recently pretended were an illusion will now return to haunt you, and, by the 20th, as Venus makes a notable aspect to Uranus, you might feel the unpredictable about to take you on: a dynamic and sudden change in a relationship, or a new romance to suit your idealistic dream. You despise upheavals and emotional conflict, but you are adaptable and generally will ride through storms and come out the other side unscathed, often leaving the past tied neatly in a package behind you. This month you may have to weather such a frontal system and, although you may feel that you never had time to analyse the situation, and therefore control it, someone had to take the blame for losing or winning. To know that there is an answer to every problem, and to give more time to find the truth behind any imperfection can only make love a better and more positive force to be reckoned with. The year could end with the most perfect solution to all your worries and fears!

Virgo

BIRTHDAY PREDICTIONS

24th August – Any barriers that you have recently felt were built between you and love should finally break down this year and allow you to discover a new ideal.

25th August – This year should give you the time to take a hard and long look at the real aspects of any emotional involvement and realise what is required of your conviction.

26th August – Inhibitions about expressing your love may be finally brought down this year, and you have the chance to communicate more openly and with it receive genuine feelings.

27th August – However conventional you like your life to be, this year looks set to offer new and more bizarre challenges with even tame partners!

28th August – 1995 should bring your social life more into focus, although you prefer less company it could bring you the ideal you are searching for.

29th August – The purity of a relationship may finally be brought into focus this year with accurate and enticing results.

30th August – This year locked doors may be opened, and old and inferior ones well and truly closed!

31st August – Discriminating between what you love and what you need will become of major significance to you this year with exacting results.

1st September – A year when you can relax your mental activity and now begin to concentrate on close friends and partners.

2nd September – Any analysis of the truth is better than none, and this year you should have good grounds at last to see love grow.

3rd September – Working at love and emotions could this year be changed to a more playful and happier set of rules!

4th September – Freedom of expression is something you often lack, but this year may find you can offer words that are in line with your heart.

5th September – Struggles in any past relationships could now be resolved, and you may realise you have more to share than you thought!

6th September – This may be the year when you allow acquaintances to turn into genuine and trustworthy friends, rather than keeping your distance.

7th September – Looking for the perfect love can often elude you, but this year, if you chose to express your feelings, you may be presently surprised.

8th September – A renewed energy to communicate more openly and to criticise less should make one relationship feel charged with happiness this year.

9th September – Never doubt your need to improve on others faults, but this year let love take over where coldness usually hides.

10th September – You are often modest in words, and also in love, but this year take advantage of feeling and let yourself flow into emotion.

11th September – A long-term relationship may well take up all your time this year, but the commitment and purpose will all be worthwhile.

12th September – A year when you can be sure that partners and loved ones will always back you 100 per cent in any endeavour.

13th September – A wonderful year for your quiet but active social life to form new friends and closer companions, and maybe even a light romance.

14th September – Love will enter your heart this year if you desire it, but fault-finding can only lead to a colder spirit.

15th September – Your support and commitment to friends and partners is unparalleled, but this year take a break and pamper yourself for a change.

16th September – You may feel that inwardly you are never satisfied in your search for perfect love, but this year you may encounter pure romance without even knowing it!

17th September – Your ideals are high, and if you allow others to express their feelings, you may be pleasantly surprised how your own heart opens too.

18th September – Never doubt your ability to analyse and to discriminate, and this year use it to its full and powerful advantage in all matters of love.

19th September – Happiness is only what you make it, and this year you should be able to put all your mental energy into achieving it.

20th September – This year sees romance and your high ideals gather a new strength and with it a new long-term commitment.

21st September – A harmonious year, when not only friends and family will support your commitments, but partners may grow closer than ever before.

22nd September – Only you can know that perfection is truly in someone's eyes. And this year you may be lucky enough to glimpse the true love, if you look hard enough.

23rd September – Passion is not high on your list for romantic happiness, but you may have to contend with it to enjoy this year's emotional stability.